TOWN HOUSE CONVERSIONS

HOUSE & GARDEN BOOK OF

TOWN HOUSE CONVERSIONS

A PRACTICAL GUIDE BY JOYCE LOWRIE ARIBA

COLLINS – LONDON & GLASGOW in association with THE CONDÉ NAST PUBLICATIONS LTD

Published by COLLINS – LONDON & GLASGOW
in association with THE CONDÉ NAST PUBLICATIONS LTD
COPYRIGHT © 1972 THE CONDÉ NAST PUBLICATIONS LTD
ISBN 0 00 435078 2
Printed in Great Britain for the Publishers by
Hazell, Watson & Viney Ltd.,
Aylesbury, Bucks.

CONTENTS

Acknowledgments: The following photographers are represented: Morley Baer, Boucher, Michael Boys, Emmett Bright, John Brookes, Peter Coats, Dan Cruickshank, Charles Dixon, Richard Einzig, Crispin Eurich, Fouquet, William Grigsby, Heller, Keystone Press, Robert Lautman, Lennard, Tom Leonard, James Mortimer, Michel Nahmias, Michael Newton, Christine Otterwill, Pinto/Primois, Louis Reens, Jasmine Rose-Innes, Stella Samuel, Henk Snoek, Marilyn Stafford, Jessica Strang, Tim Street-Porter, Barry Weller, Colin Westwood, Michael Wickham, Ray Williams, John Wingrove. Plans drawn by Michael Burrell.

INTRODUCTION

It is not only the outstanding squares and terraces of our towns and cities which need our protection. We are learning, too late almost, about the degree to which quite modest domestic buildings of the past make a civilizing contribution to the urban scene. However small and seemingly unimportant the house you take on, its existing architectural idiom deserves respect and consideration, and it can be said that the more modest the building, the more vulnerable it is to careless handling.

This is not to argue for preservation at all costs. Clearly one does not want, nor would it be practical, to preserve all old buildings as frozen monuments to the past. Unless the spaces and elements of the interior are of outstanding architectural merit, it is reasonable that they should be altered or completely renovated to suit the manner in which we want to live today. As the illustrations in this book show, it is in this area that the imagination and structural expertise of current architects have made such an outstanding contribution – releasing the rooms inside these old houses from their former box-like rigidity to reveal new and exciting possibilities of light and space.

The inside of the house is our private domain and it is reasonable that we should use it in a way that suits and pleases us best. But the way in which we treat the outside of the house is another matter, and does demand the practice of good neighbourliness. The essential character of too many old houses has been irretrievably destroyed by misdirected attempts at modernization. The clumsy alteration of one house can ruin the rhythm and balance, not only of the house itself, but of the entire street.

To take on the conversion of an old building involves certain responsibilities. Houses are in such short supply that to rescue old property of any kind is obviously well worth doing. But it is not enough simply to give an old building a new lease of life. From the moment the building becomes yours you have it in your hands, whether you realize it or not, to make a personal contribution towards improving the environment.

Careful restoration and conversion by architect Malcolm Andrews has brought a derelict Georgian house back to life as a family home

7

THE HUNT

With the current boom in property, house-hunting has become a thoroughly cut-throat business. Not only do you have to be quick off the mark, because there are bound to be other people breathing down your neck, but once having decided that you want the place, there are the additional obstacles such as surveys, mortgages and the hazards of gazumping to be met before it is safely yours. Many of these problems can be overcome, however, if you prepare yourself thoroughly beforehand.

I have had two separate experiences of buying a town house. Being an architect gives me an edge over many people in that I can see more quickly what might be made workable but, apart from that aspect, the process is pretty much the same as it would be for anyone else. One longs to be able to reveal a magic short-cut. It is not enough to have a large balance at the bank: a well-planned campaign is essential however much money you have, and is even more important if you are short of cash.

The first step is to pinpoint areas that appear to suit your family's particular needs and then to buy large detailed maps of the areas that seem to be workable possibilities. Each family will have its own special requirements: convenient public transport to avoid parking problems; schools nearby; a hospital for a member of the family which needs regular out-patient treatment; some green space nearby for walks on summer evenings; interesting shopping, perhaps an open market; a good public library.

This sort of investigation is essential because no house, however attractive and functional in itself, in the end will make up for being so inconveniently placed that friends are discouraged from visiting, and shopping for more than the bare necessities means a long car or bus ride.

At the same time, you need to have an open mind. So many districts that were near slums a few years ago are now fashionable and sought-after. The clever thing is to stay one jump ahead of the speculators and get in before prices start to rocket. The present hysterical demand for houses is bound to continue for some years and any district with good bus and train services to the town or city centre, or near some pleasant green space, river or canal, or where there are sizable pockets of family-sized Regency or early-Victorian houses, will inevitably be discovered in its turn. Just one house imaginatively painted, is often enough to make other people aware of the street's possibilities.

Once you have bought a large-scale map of a district and begun to study it, you will be amazed at how many charming tucked-away streets and cul-de-sacs still exist in an undiscovered state. Canals and river banks are always worth exploring and there are often small parks known only to the immediate locals. Even churchyards and allotments provide welcome fresh air.

Just as one needs to be open-minded and flexible about the kind of district one settles in, one needs to be equally open-minded about the sort of house one wants. Only the very rich can afford to be specific, but I don't think this need be counted as an advantage, as flexibility can open up all sorts of rewarding possibilities. When you go house-hunting, you need to consider future possibilities as well as present requirements, such as babies growing up in need of their own bed-sitting-rooms, or elderly parents coming to live with you and needing a small, self-contained flat. If the district is a convenient one and you think you would be reluctant to leave a garden worked on for years, it is worth questioning whether the house could sub-divide comfortably when the time comes for children to leave home and the accommodation becomes unnecessarily large.

Imagination and courage lead to dividends when it comes to property and the older and shabbier the property (provided, of course, it is not an exquisite period house in a fashionable district), the more space inside the house and the more garden will you get for your money – and space is one of today's greatest luxuries.

The fabric of an old house will always require more attention than a recently-built one, but once the main work of modernization has been properly done, re-roofing, damp-proofing, plumbing, electrics, and so on, the rest is quite often of a scale that the layman can tackle.

Really large houses are frequently much less expensive, space for space, than their smaller neighbours and it is worth considering one for sub-division in any district where there is a shortage of accommodation. A university town is a case in point. However, some loans do put conditions on sub-letting and this is a point that should be investigated when assessing which form of mortgage would suit you best.

It is useful to be able to assess the general suitability of a house before going to the expense of calling in a surveyor or architect to look it over for you. You have to learn from the beginning not to be dismayed by dirt and clutter, and to see beyond the peeling paint, festooning wallpaper and sagging roof. So long as the trouble has not gone too far, dampness can be cured, woodworm treated, floors resurfaced, roofs made good – white paint can work miracles with the all-pervading gloom. Crumbling outhouses and back extensions can be trimmed back to reduce rates and maintenance expenses and perhaps provide some building material for other work – more substantial ones might have additional floors added. A garage, or space for one, is always a tremendous asset in a central area. Easy access for tradesmen, fuel storage and space for dustbins are also important. Basements are no longer considered a disadvantage when getting mortgages and can be put to so many uses, and even bring in an income. Making them dry is no problem these days.

Brick and stone walls are the easiest and cheapest to maintain. Unless it is the only way to rescue the appearance of a house, it is best to avoid having to paint it because of the maintenance expense it can involve. If painting is the only remedy, however, there are now one or two finishes that are virtually permanent, although expensive.

Once you have earmarked a few possible districts, it is advisable to go to the different local authorities concerned to see what planning proposals they have for the district. This is an essential precaution as unscrupulous people may get news of some development that will reduce the value of their property and try to get rid of it to some unsuspecting buyer desperate for a house before the plans are made public. These future plans – a school perhaps, a factory, road widening – may mean at worst demolition of the house; at best, noise, dust and smells which will spoil the amenities and decrease the value of the property. Your solicitor should uncover such proposals when he starts his searches, but by then a lot of time and fees could have been wasted.

After finding a house you risk losing it if you cannot find anyone to give you a loan quickly enough; it is as well to explore all the mortgage possibilities before doing any actual house-hunting. Building societies, insurance companies, and sometimes banks all lend money against houses. Terms and conditions vary considerably and you need to find out what would suit your own circumstances. The Consumer Association's *Money Which?* has published useful comparative surveys on these three methods of borrowing money which anyone thinking of buying a house, and needing a mortgage to do it, would find useful reading.

As it becomes increasingly clear when you are searching that those able to make a quick decision win the prizes, it is also advisable to gather together a team of friendly professionals who would be ready to act on your behalf immediately a really good thing came up. You will need a solicitor with a reputation for being experienced and quick at conveyancing. If you are planning a move to a town or city some distance away, there is a case for finding a local firm of solicitors as they will know the area and have useful contacts. You should also find a builder ready to give an outline estimate of any work that had to be done and have a surveyor or architect standing by who you know will give you a reliable but not conservative opinion of the structure of any property you like.

With your team of experts ready, you can then tackle the agents. The professional bodies of estate agents will give you the names of reputable firms operating locally. Be prepared to attack on every front, telephoning half-a-dozen agents regularly every week, following up advertisements in the local and national presses, and asking local tradesmen.

Another way of tracking down houses, is to go to the local authority and find out who owns the rather run-down and seedy house on the corner of a street you like. Some have used this method with successful results; in one case, the absentee landlord was an old lady living in Bognor who had let the house out as furnished rooms and was glad to be free of the responsibility involved in rent collection and house maintenance.

It is even worth taking up a house with statutory tenants. You will certainly get it a lot cheaper this way and it needn't affect your putting it in order, installing new plumbing and electric wiring, etc, ready for the time you can take it over completely. However, it is essential to find out what the tenants are like before you commit yourself or you could encounter unforseen difficulties.

If you are fairly adventurous and prepared to have some work done on the property, it is worth looking around for disused warehouses. Docks anywhere offer exciting possibilities, and sometimes one can find an isolated shop which has the bonus of already having an opened-up space. In one instance a house with what had been a clinic linked to it, made an interesting conversion. The waiting-room became a splendidly large and interestingly-lit living-room with the dispensary off it providing a dining/kitchen. One can sometimes even find a dis-used chapel, an old school or Victorian office block. In New York, for example, the old Bell Telephone Company has been transformed by a group of architects into a block of stunning studio flats. The thing to do is to look for space. Local authorities in town seem readier to consider giving planning permission to turn such buildings into living accommodation than are many rural authorities.

Some people even drop letters through the doors of any suitable house in the streets they particularly like, on the chance that the owners are thinking of selling in the near future. It can also help to establish yourself in a district you like by moving into a stop-gap flat so that you can keep your ear to the ground more easily.

CLINCHING THE DEAL

The best way of ensuring that you get the house you want at a price you can afford is to have a body of first class professionals or experts lined up behind you. You need to tell these specialists – estate agent, surveyor or architect (depending on how much converting you propose to do), solicitor, builder and, possibly, garden designer – exactly what you are looking for, how much money you've got to spend and how much converting you are prepared to take on, so that they are ready to move immediately you say the word.

First of all, you will need to choose an estate agent. It is better to deal only with those firms who are members of one of the professional bodies – the Chartered Auctioneers and Estate Agents Institute, the Chartered Land Agents Society and the Incorporated Society of Auctioneers and Landed Property Agents – as they are bound to respect professional ethics and, should you be let down in any way, you have a powerful means with which to complain.

In dealing with an estate agent, the buyer pays nothing to the agent unless he asks the firm to advertise on his behalf for a particular sort of house. Otherwise, it is the seller who pays the agent's fees. You should always tell an agent precisely what you are looking for, and make it clear if you are prepared to tackle a building in a really rough state or if you want to limit the improvements to renewing the services, redecoration and putting in a new bathroom and kitchen perhaps. Half done-up houses can be a problem, especially if you haven't money to spare. You will find yourself agonizing over whether or not to rip out things you don't like the look of, but are perfectly adequate, when there are several more important things to be done. If you are really adventurous, and are game to take on an old warehouse or shop, let your estate agent know. And, once you have found yourself a good firm, be importunate.

Houses are sold in one of two ways – either by private treaty or by auction. Property can be sold by private treaty either through an agent or directly from the owner himself. As it is so easy to sell property these days, some people feel they can save themselves an agent's fees and advertise their home themselves in the national and local press. A house bought in this way could be cheaper than one bought through an agent.

The auctioning of property is usually organized by a firm of estate agents and auctioneers. Buying by auction is much more popular than it used to be as house prices have risen at such a rate that people, and indeed estate agents, with property to sell are uncertain of what in fact is a reasonable price to ask. It takes rather more confidence to buy at an auction as there are none of the stages, as in a private treaty, which give you a chance to change your mind before completion. With auctioned property, the contract is embodied in the conditions of sale and these conditions are printed on the brochure describing the property. If you are interested in a building that is to be sold by auction, it is essential that your solicitor checks carefully its conditions of sale and their implications, and that your surveyor thoroughly examines the structure before the day of the auction. If you make the highest bid and haven't withdrawn it before the hammer falls for the last time, you will have made a binding contract from which you cannot withdraw. The only situation that lets you out of the contract is for it to be discovered that the vendor in fact hadn't the right to sell.

With all your enquiries made, you can safely join the bidding. Quite often, a reserve price is put on the house which gives a bottom limit to its possible price and if this price isn't reached, the auctioneer on behalf of the vendor is at liberty to withdraw the property from the sale. Should your bid be the highest, you wait until the end of the auction to sign the Memorandum of Contract, paying the auctioneer a deposit of 10 per cent. The auctioneer acts as agent to both parties and is entitled to sign the Memorandum on your behalf if you leave the sale before signing it.

Once the hammer falls at an auction, you can feel that the property is safely yours. Buying a property by private treaty, however, is a lengthier process, as both you and the vendor can withdraw before the deal is completed. It used to be considered bad practice for the vendor to do this but the present demand for property has encouraged vendors to put up their price mid-way through a sale if they find someone else who is prepared to make a higher offer. This is what is known as gazumping and, as I write, there is no legal protection for the would-be purchaser, although there is a lot of concern about it. Sometimes this buyer is given the opportunity to better his original offer; sometimes he finds that the property has been snatched away without him being given a chance to make a higher bid. This is where a reputable estate agent and a shrewd solicitor can be of considerable help.

When property is sold by private treaty, the procedure goes something like this. Your solicitor makes an offer, *subject to survey and contract*. These are the words which protect you, should you subsequently discover that the structure is in a state of near collapse or that a neighbour has a right-of-way through your garden to his garage (a case of which I heard recently) or that there is some disadvantage which you find unacceptable. So never sign a document which does not include them. At this stage, it is usual to pay out a deposit of 10 per cent of the purchase price. You can pay this directly through the estate agent, or through your solicitor to protect you from any possibility of unscrupulousness on the agent's part. At the same time, you should contact whoever you hope to obtain a mortgage from and ask them to arrange for their surveyor to check over the building. You should also arrange for your own surveyor or architect to look over the property for you. If the structure turns out to be in a worse state than you had thought, the clause 'subject to survey and contract' allows you to withdraw from negotiations and ask for the return of your deposit.

While these surveys are being carried out and a mortgage negotiated, your solicitor will be making his searches, that is, checking whether the present owner really has the right to sell the property to you and whether there are any restrictive conditions which affect the use of the property, if the local authority is developing the area in a way which could reduce its value or if any rights-of-way, rights-of-light, etc, exist which could mean an intrusion of your privacy. While your solicitor is carrying out these searches, the vendor's solicitor is preparing the contract.

Once the mortgage people have agreed to a loan, your surveyor has given a satisfactory report and your solicitor has found no insuperable problems, contracts are exchanged between the two solicitors. Your solicitor checks the contract's conditions to see that your interests are properly safeguarded, which is why you should never share a solicitor with the person from whom you are buying. You and the vendor sign a copy of the contract and then exchange copies. If the property is to be owned jointly, both husband and wife must sign the contract. This is something you should discuss with your solicitor, as it affects the death duties to be paid, should one of you die before the other.

The contract is now binding, although the person selling the house still has to maintain the property until the actual conveyance is made. The conveyance is the deed under which the ownership of the property passes to you. During this period, the responsibility of insuring the property becomes yours and you have to be allowed reasonable access to it. On completion day, the solicitors meet to sign and seal the documents. Your solicitor is handed the deeds of the property unless a loan is involved, in which case they go to the mortgagee's solicitor. A banker's draft for the balance of the purchase price is handed over by your solicitor and the property is yours. Unless any problems arise, a solicitor skilled in conveyancing can get a sale through in about three weeks.

The property you buy may be registered or unregistered, depending on how recently it has changed hands. When it has a registered title, the ownership will be recorded either at the Central Land Registry or in certain district registries. Some people think they can save solicitor's fees by handling the legal side of the transaction themselves, but I would not recommend this in cases when a property is unregistered as it can easily mean searching through letters and documents extending back over a considerable number of years, and without professional experience you may well find yourself in trouble. There are so many things involved – rights-of-access, rights-of-light or boundaries which could limit what you can do with the building subsequently – that it is safer to call in an expert. Otherwise, you could even find that you had no right to the building at all, as it might be discovered later that the person you bought it from had no claim to ownership.

With a registered property, however, the complications of the search are removed and you may feel you could negotiate the purchase without calling in a solicitor. If you do decide to do it yourself, you should buy a copy of *The Legal Side of Buying a House* (a Consumers' Association publication) which will take you step by step through the entire procedure.

Whether you go it alone or employ a solicitor, the following points should be established at the outset of your negotiations:

1. The address of the property and how it is shown on an attached plan.
2. Full name of the vendor.
3. The price of the property.
4. The amount of the deposit and whether it has been paid to the vendor's solicitors.
5. How long will completion take?
6. How and where is the title registered?
7. Whether the adjoining roads are maintained at public or private expense.
8. How the area is zoned and what proposals there are for re-development?
9. Description of main and rain-water drainage, details of the water, gas, and electricity services available and whether these, or the main drainage, cross other people's property – if they do, are any conditions attached?
10. Are there any restrictive covenants?
11. What do annual outgoings amount to?
12. When will insurance be your liability?
13. Details of the mortgage.

An act of Parliament has established solictors' fees for buying and selling property and it is this scale that most solicitors work to, unless the transaction involves considerably more work through unexpected difficulties. Bills for out-of-pocket expenses, such as staying overnight at an hotel and travelling, can also be added to the solicitor's account. Your solicitor will be able to give you a rough estimate of what his charges are likely to be once he knows the price of the house. For a house costing £10,000, investigating the title, approving the contract, preparing and completing the conveyance, would cost around £105. Roughly a third less would be chargeable in the case of a registered title. Your solicitor will charge you an additional fee if you are negotiating a mortgage for approving the document which creates it, and you would also have to pay a fee to the mortgagee's solicitor at the same time. For property costing over £10,000, stamp duty is charged as well.

If you need to borrow capital to buy the house, whoever lends you the money will want the building surveyed first to see whether it represents a safe investment and you will have to pay for this survey. Sometimes the result of this survey is available to the buyer, sometimes not. You may wonder why it is necessary for both the mortgage company and for you to retain a surveyor, especially as you have to pay for both the surveys. This is because the mortgage company is simply concerned with recovering its investment in the property should you, for some reason, find yourself unable to meet your repayments, when it would be up to them to resell the building. You need to have the building surveyed to assess in detail the state of its structure, services, decoration and so on, so that you can make some kind of assessment of how much you will have to pay to have it put right.

If you are willing to take on a fairly decrepit building, because you like the prospect of reshaping it to suit yourself, make sure you let your surveyor know so that he can bear it in mind when assessing the property's value for you. In such a case, you may well find it better sense to employ an architect rather than a surveyor to check over the building for you. Although a surveyor can design structures, he is not a designer in the aesthetic sense. His concern is stability. He is the right person to call in if you propose to keep the house pretty much as it stands, doing little more than, say, re-wiring, re-plumbing and re-decorating. An architect is equally experienced so far as the structure of a building is concerned but can, in addition, see possibilities in a house and garden that enable him to advise you in a rather more constructive fashion. Even if it is simply a matter of some additional windows, he will ensure that they blend in with the character of the existing ones and with the façade generally.

If you are looking for a building that will need such extensive re-making that ultimately you will need an architect to help you, this argues for finding a suitable one before you start house-hunting so that he can survey any likely property that comes up.

If you do employ an architect, it is as well to be sure that he is, in fact, a qualified one. For a person to call himself an architect, he has to be registered with the Architects' Registration Council. Some designers who are not fully trained and qualified architects practise under the title of architectural designers which can deceive the unwary. Their work may well be attractive, but they will not be bound by the same professional disciplines as an architect and, in the event of their mishandling the job, you will have no redress. Finding and employing an architect is discussed fully in the next section.

Should you feel a surveyor to be adequate for your needs, your solicitor or estate agent may be able to recommend one. Otherwise, the Secretary of the Royal Institute of Chartered Surveyors will send you a list of those practising in the area. No set scale of fees is laid down by the Institute for survey work of this kind. The standing of the firm of surveyors, the degree of detail required and the scale of the job will all govern what is charged. A thorough inspection and a full report on a four storeyed terraced house could cost £100, a less detailed one as little as £30.

How to get a mortgage

There are several ways of raising a mortgage: some suit certain types of property better than others, some suit particular incomes, and it is worth investigating all of them, especially when you are buying your first house.

You should work out how high a mortgage you can afford. The usual rule of thumb is two-and-a-half times your income. If you are in a safe job (Civil Service, say) or can establish your prospects, the proportion may be raised to three times your salary. Generally, this is computed on the husband's income, although occasionally the wife's is taken into account as well: married women usually have difficulties establishing themselves as wage-earners since mortgagees feel that, if they are still young enough to have children, they may at any time find themselves pregnant and then stop work. As a rule, monthly payments should not exceed one week's salary.

You will also need ready cash not only for decorating and equipping the house but for the deposit, the legal expenses, and the difference between the mortgage you obtain and the actual price of the house.

Many people use solicitors or brokers to negotiate their mortgages for them. With insurance policy mortgages and private trust mortgages, this is essential; but with local authority mortgages, bank mortgages and, in most cases, building society mortgages, you can do the negotiating yourselves. It's worth presenting yourself in as business-like a manner as possible. List your assets: your present income and job prospects, 'expectations', covenants due to mature, valuable possessions, etc. Detail how you intend to improve the property and thus add to its value. It is a help here to employ an architect to work out some drawings, even if you intend to supervise or carry out the work yourself.

If money is short, it is sometimes an advantage to apply at the beginning of the financial year. Most institutions have a certain amount to lend and it is usually a case of first come, first served, until the funds are used up.

Nearly 80 per cent of mortgages are raised from building societies. The type of property these societies prefer is the uncomplicated low-priced house built since 1920. They may lend up to 95 per cent of their valuation of the property and the period of loan is usually up to 25 years. Usually the rate of interest is that recommended by the Building Societies' Association.

The advantage of borrowing from a building society is that it is a straightforward way of raising a mortgage on a house built during the last 50 years. It is traditionally the best buy for lower-income people who cannot claim all the tax concessions permitted on an insurance company mortgage.

However, with a building society loan it is necessary to get permission for letting or sub-letting; they will not consider flats, other than purpose-built ones, or short leases; and they are reluctant to include the wife's contribution to the family income for more than a short period.

The Building Societies' Association will help you with information and suggest you interview the individual building society's local manager, before you actually find a house, to work out the sort of loan he might give you. Although the usual ceiling of a loan is two-and-a-half times your income, the terms offered can vary which is why some people employ solicitors and brokers to advise them on which society to use. It is worth remembering that societies are always kinder to people who have previously deposited some money with them.

In the case of an insurance company mortgage, the company pay over the agreed amount (a proportion of their valuation of the property) and, for the period of the loan, you pay them interest on this – but not the capital. The capital is taken care of by a life insurance or endowment policy which is designed to mature at the end of the mortgage: you also pay premiums on this policy.

Insurance companies will consider older, more unusual and often more expensive property than building societies, and they will consider flats. They will lend up to 80–90 per cent of their valuation for a period of up to thirty years, and the rate of interest varies between companies.

If you pay enough tax at the standard rate to take full advantage of tax concessions (because you are paying only interest and insurance premiums both of which are allowable) you pay in the end very much less than you do for any other type of mortgage – especially if you pay slightly larger premiums for a 'with profits' policy. Also you are automatically insured, so if you die the house is not outstanding. With other forms of mortgage, this can only be achieved by taking out a mortgage protection policy: however, the cost is low and it is an essential precaution.

A mortgage with an insurance company is not worth it if you do not expect within the next 20 years to be able to claim all the tax benefits. The rate of interest is increased if you let or sub-let all or a part of the property and most insurance companies are reluctant for you to do this. If this sort of loan interests you, take advice from an insurance broker, or go to see your solicitor or bank manager. They will also be able to tell you which building societies arrange insurance-type mortgages.

In the case of a local authority mortgage, there will be a slight difference in policy from others. Local authorities will consider older and more unusual property than building societies, and they are interested in conversions that could mean the provision of several living units where there has formerly only been one. The proportion of the valuation they will lend varies again, but some lend 100 per cent on certain properties. The period of loan is up to 30 years and the rate of interest varies with the bank rate and between different authorities.

Some local authorities give you a more realistic valuation of the property than other bodies which lend money, and so allow you a larger sum, and they are prepared to lend against short leases and flats. Local authorities do not object to you letting some of the house unfurnished or even furnished for short periods, although they may set a limit on the rent. Sometimes, on older property, the council makes it a condition of the loan that certain improvements are made, and may withhold some money until the work has been done. The problem is that the machinery for getting a council to agree to the loan can take longer than with other forms of mortgage, and this may prejudice your chances if there is competition for a particular property.

To find out about local authority loans you simply telephone or visit the local town or county hall and fill in an application form, but if you want to make improvements and qualify for a larger loan, these have to be detailed.

Whether your bank will give you a loan to buy a house depends on the current financial situation: in a credit squeeze it is seldom worth expecting large long-term loans. But policies do differ from bank to bank, even from branch to branch. If your family fortunes are attached to one particular branch, it is well worth approaching the manager there, especially if a senior member of your family is prepared to act as some sort of guarantor.

Banks will lend up to 100 per cent of the purchase price and make no conditions as to the character of the property, sub-letting or the character of the alterations. However, they do not like their money tied up for long periods and the most you could hope for would be ten years in which to repay. The rate of interest charged is usually one to two per cent above the current bank rate. The bank does not usually hold the title as a building society does, but the deeds are deposited with them for security. When you go to see the bank manager, it is particularly important to be well briefed on the property, possible outgoings, incomings, and how you will repay the loan, etc. You may not be able to obtain a mortgage from the bank, but you can very often get a short-term loan from six to nine months to help you buy a second house before you sell the first, or, alternatively, to repair a dilapidated house so that it qualifies for a more generous mortgage.

If you are not successful in arranging a mortgage in any other way, your solicitor, bank manager or insurance broker may be able to arrange a private mortgage for you. Trustees of private trust funds are sometimes prepared to lend money from these funds. There is usually a limit of two thirds of an independent valuation of the property and there is no set rate of interest. The period of the loan is arranged between the two parties and is usually shorter than a building society, insurance company or local authority would allow.

You should try to have a clause in the covenant which will prevent the lender calling for repayment at short notice. It is often possible to get a loan on older or more unusual property by borrowing in this way and you are also free to negotiate terms on such things as sub-letting and alterations.

If you have several friends who are house-hunting as well, investigate the possibilities offered by joining forces and becoming a housing association. It is a great advantage if the group includes an architect and lawyer among its members. The people to discuss this with are The National Federation of Housing Associations. The loan is arranged together with improvement grants with the local authority – the term of the mortgage is usually 30 years and can cover 100 per cent of the costs.

The Option Mortgage Scheme is designed to help people who do not pay tax at the standard rate as they do not benefit from tax rebate in the way that those who pay tax at the standard rate do. If you think this scheme might help you, there is a leaflet describing it fully, obtainable from your local Citizens' Advice Bureau, council offices or any building society office.

GETTING STARTED

Because of the high cost of town property, it is the best practice from every point of view to do the conversion job as well as possible. This doesn't mean gold-plating the taps, but it does mean working from the outside in, getting the structural skin into sound weather-proof order, providing an adequate and appropriate central heating system and good insulation, choosing fittings and finishes and so on that will be maintenance-free for as long as possible. It is worth getting as much amenity and spatial value as you can from the property – both house and garden. How to set about doing this is discussed in detail in later sections. Fitted carpets and hand-printed wallpapers can come later, but, if you don't see to the structural part at the beginning, you will always regret it. With building costs spiralling, the more you can get done at the beginning, the cheaper it will be in the long run.

Mortgage companies relate what they will lend you to the way you propose to improve the property, and it is for this reason that it is worth going to an architect. It is quite possible to save his fees from the amount he will save you by supervising the job well. The best way to find an architect is to talk to friends who have had similar work done and whose houses you like, or take a magazine, such as *House & Garden* and follow up the names of architects whose work appeals to you. Failing that, you can go to the local public library and consult the current Royal Institute of British Architects' Directory of Practices (RIBA). It lists architects by areas, along with examples of recent projects. If possible, go to see some of the work to be sure you like it. Solicit the help of RIBA's regional office (telephone directory yellow pages under *Architects*) or the Clients' Bureau of RIBA, giving details of the conversion, locality, possible costs, etc.

Sir Henry Wotton says in his *Elements of Architecture*, first published in London in 1624:

> *In Architecture as in all other Operative Arts, the end must direct the Operation. The end is to build well. Well, building hath three Conditions: commoditie, firmeness, and delight.*

An architect is both a practical man and artist. He ensures that you have efficient services and equipment, appropriate materials and a thoroughly sound structure. But, more than this, his imaginative interpretation of your needs can result not only in a remarkably easy-to-run house but in relationships of materials, colours and spaces that can feed back visual pleasure and delight.

It is extremely important that you find your architect personally sympathetic. You are going to see a lot of him for some nine months or so, and you will have to be prepared to reveal a great deal about yourselves and the way you want to live if he is to do a really successful job for you. If you find after the first one or two meetings that you haven't started to establish a rapport, it may be better to consider employing someone else. But, having taken on an architect, it is necessary to write a formal letter stating that you wish to terminate the arrangement and pay his fees to date before another architect can take up the work. A registered architect is bound by rules of professional conduct which are published in a booklet *Conditions of Engagement*, available from RIBA Publications Ltd, 66 Portman Place, London W1. These conditions include the minimum fees for which members of the RIBA may undertake work and describe the professional services which clients may expect in return. The architect you take on will give you a copy, but it is worth obtaining this booklet before that to see to what you will be committed. Send, too, for a copy of *Services of an Architect* and *Working with your Architect*.

Work, such as structural surveys and general advice on the possibilities of a building, is charged at an hourly rate, the minimum hourly rate being £5 per hour. Travelling time and any out-of-pocket expenses, such as hotels and train fares or mileage allowance for cars, will also be charged for. Work to existing buildings is charged for on a percentage basis as follows:

Total Construction Cost	Minimum % Rate	Minimum Charge
Up to £2,500	13·0	—
£2,500–£8,000	12.5	£325.00
£8,000–£14,000	12·0	£1,000.00

A proportion of the fee is payable at each work stage.

In calling in an architect, you delegate a lot of worries. He takes over full responsibility for getting through planning approvals and ensuring that the structural work meets Building Regulations. Not only will he investigate the possibility of obtaining a local council grant, but he will also find builders, a heating engineer of contractor, and, if necessary, he will be able to put you in touch with a garden designer. He should also be well-versed in the latest domestic equipment, floor and wall-finishes and so on.

If you don't want to spend more than £1,000 on alterations and repairs, you may feel you can manage without an architect or surveyor and deal with the builder yourself. In this case, it is even more important to find a good builder. This is easier said than done, but it really is better to pay a little more to have a reliable pleasant firm dealing with the job. Ask friends and acquaintances which firms they have had good work from, or, if you are going to a completely new district, the local authority will often let you have the names of reputable firms in the area. Don't go to very large firms for a small job – they will charge more and are less likely to take as much interest in you as small firms will. A large organization is geared for major projects and it doesn't really pay them to do small ones. However, some large firms do have a small works department which is equipped to deal with small-scale jobs.

You must first decide exactly what work you wish to have done and the maximum sum you will be able to spend on it. A proportion of this figure, say 5 to 10 per cent, should be set aside to take care of contingencies.

If the work involves any alterations to the structure of the building, you will have to explain these proposals to the Local Borough Engineer and the Local Planning Officer to discover if they are in any way contrary to Building Laws or Planning Regulations. If such regulations are contravened, the penalties can be quite heavy. Instruct your builder to state in his estimate that he has allowed for arrangements for the inspection of the work by the interested authorities and will see that it is carried out.

Never let a builder start work before giving you an estimate. It is always worth trying to get competitive quotations from firms of equal standing. The problem is that small builders who are any good are generally so busy that many are reluctant to take time off to make out a detailed estimate unless they are sure of the job. You must send the builders as detailed a description as possible of the work you want done, either in trades or room-by-room. You must give them the name, make, size, colour, etc, of every fitting and finish. You should also provide simple plans and elevations showing the sizes and positions of everything you want built in or fixed. It doesn't matter that these are not expert so long as they make it clear that, say, the top of the bookshelves has to be lined up with the top of the mantelpiece, or the skirting has to be continued round to form a plinth for some cupboards.

Having decided on the details of the work to be done, two or three builders of equal calibre should be invited to submit tenders for the work. You should ask them to state:
1. The make and quality of materials they will use.
2. That all work will conform to Building Regulations and Planning Requirements. That, if necessary, they will apply for approvals

for the above on your behalf and for Standard or Discretionary Grants if the work is eligible for one.

3. That all work will be made good on completion.
4. That, when the work calls for it, a maintenance period of six months will be allowed for.
5. The starting and finishing dates.
6. The terms upon which payment is requested.
7. The prices of the individual sections of the work.
8. That only extras and variations for which written authority is obtained will be charged for.
9. That arrangements will be made for the care of any existing valuable materials, such as lead, slate or marble and other fittings such as doors, door furniture, etc, which are capable of re-use.
10. Where work involves excavation, both sub-soil and topsoil shall be deposited only where the client directs.

British Standards cover most building materials, and a request that all materials shall comply with the appropriate Standard of the Institute or to a pattern approved by the Water, Gas or Electricity Boards will ensure that materials are not sub-standard goods at lower prices.

It is usual on large-scale works to arrange for a series of part payments, and an estimate priced in some detail is useful as it enables part payments to be related to the progress of the work. They should be made promptly, as in handling the capital at his disposal, a builder may rely to some extent on them, for when they are delayed it can cause inconvenience and possibly loss. Some money, though, should always be kept back to ensure a satisfactory completion. If a maintenance period is arranged, a further agreed sum should be held back until the expiration of the period and any maintenance work has been executed.

The estimate should be studied carefully to see that all the items are included and any omissions should be confirmed with the builder in writing and not verbally.

As there are some building operations for which it is difficult to prepare an estimate, the builder may quote on a cost-plus basis. When this occurs, the allowance for contingencies in the original budget should be increased and, if possible, an assurance obtained from the builder that the charge will not exceed a given figure.

Although the lowest tender may be the most tempting, it is not always the best choice and should be examined with care unless the firm has a reliable reputation. Some builders work on the principle 'get the job and make it pay on the extras', and it is on conversions and alterations that extras can accumulate if the work is not planned and estimated on a sound basis.

A well-planned job should not have additions, variations or deletions. The cost of these may come as a shock to people who order them without first finding out the price. They can be a cause of loss to the builder, too, as they are requested all too often at the wrong stage of the job to be worked into a programme economically.

You should try to visit the site once or twice a week to see how the work is going. Be prepared for the work to look rough in its unfinished state, but don't hesitate to query anything you feel anxious about. Try not to change your mind once work has started. If you do, give your instructions to the foreman, rather than the man on the job, and confirm them in writing without delay.

Don't despair too much over delays; they seem inevitable and they are by no means always due to the builder's lack of organization. Delivery of a special sink can be promised within three weeks and take three months, or a run of bad weather can put the builder behind with another job and delay starting on yours. Be friendly to the men on the job and generally you will find they will be loyal to you, but don't let your builder bully you. Take his advice by all means when it suits you, but remember that the fixtures, fittings and finishes that he recommends may be made to suit his convenience and pocket rather than the end result.

The legal position

Anyone who has had experience of building, converting, or even having minor alterations made to a house, will have been amazed and often enraged at the amount of legislation that can govern something even as simple as putting in a new window or making a minor structural alteration inside which is quite invisible from the outside.

If you are undertaking any building work that involves changing the use or external appearance of your property, any structural alterations or new plumbing installations, your local authority will want to know about it.

You may decorate to your heart's content, both inside and out (unless there is a clause in your lease forbidding it), fix tiles or shelves to your walls, fit new gutters and down pipes, replace slates and tiles, repoint brickwork and renew doors and windows, but when it comes to structural repairs, removing walls, building a new room or a garage, or installing a wash-hand basin or lavatory where there was none before, then you are legally bound to comply with certain by-laws and regulations and, in some cases, permission may be denied.

Building regulations, however, are not a recent innovation. The very earliest recorded date back as long ago as 2000 BC and are contained in the famous Laws of Hammurabi, King of Babylon. The first to appear in Britain were part of the 1189 Ordinance of Henry Fitz Ailwin, Lord Mayor of London. Among other things, these controlled the construction of party walls, privies and even the siting of buildings, but they applied only to the City of London.

Building regulations

Although these can seem maddeningly restrictive at times, the essential purpose of building regulations is to ensure that a building is safe-guarded against such hazards as structural collapse, fire, damp and rot, and that its occupants are provided with proper sanitary arrangements, space, light, ventilation, and sound and heat insulation, as well as safely-designed staircases, and so on.

It was the unprecedented expansion of our industrial towns in the nineteenth century that forced into being the Public Health and Local Government Acts of 1877 which are the basis of our present-day system.

Following the First World War, the severe shortages of building materials made officially-sponsored experiment essential and, to handle this the Building Research Station was set up at Garston, Watford, in 1921. The Codes of Practice it has produced, coupled with the work of the British Standards Institution, have helped to replace rule-of-thumb standards with those based on scientific calculation, breaking some of the former inflexibility of the by-laws by offering the regulating authorities acceptable alternatives. You should ensure that any work you have done, and materials or fittings you have, conforms to the appropriate Code of Practice or British Standard.

The old building by-laws, which varied from place to place, were superseded on 1st February, 1966, by a new set of national Building Regulations that apply throughout England and Wales, except for the area administered by the former London County Council which has its own system of Building Acts and By-laws. These new Building Regulations were brought into being to achieve uniformity and to take better account of recent changes in techniques and materials. Under them, the Minister (Public Buildings and Works) has delegated to the local authority power to dispense with or to relax certain of these regulations; a right of appeal exists if a local authority refuses to relax a regulation. If you are converting or adding to an existing house, any new work must meet the new regulations, although you will not be required to alter any existing work, unless this is a condition of the award of an improvement grant. However, if you are changing the use of a building – eg, converting a warehouse or a shop into a dwelling – then you will have to bring the whole building into line with certain of the regulations. This will also be the case if you are dividing a single family house into two or more flats.

So if you are planning any changes in your house, it is a good plan to telephone or write a note, describing what you propose, to the district surveyor's office to check whether it will be affected by Building Regulations. If you are employing an architect or surveyor, he will look after this for you. If you are handling the job on your own, you should include a clause to cover this in your instructions to the builder.

Smoke control zone

You should also check whether you are moving into a smoke-controlled zone as, under the Clean Air Act of 1956, 'the emission of smoke from chimneys constitutes an offence'. However, should you take on a property which has nothing but old-fashioned grates, you are entitled to a grant towards replacing them with a modern appliance which will burn a smokeless fuel. Advice on this can be obtained from the health department of your local authority.

Planning permission

The purpose of planning control is to prevent people from doing whatever they like to their property without regard for their neighbours' or the public's interest.

If you want to make any material changes in the outside appearance or in the use of your property (such as adding a new porch or demolishing an old one, or opening a garage drive into the road, where there was none before), or if you want to change the property's purpose (warehouse to dwelling, or even house into self-contained flats), then you will need planning permission.

When it is a small matter, perhaps a new window, your local planning department may make the decision itself, taking only a week or so about it. In the case of more extensive work, the application may have to go before the country or borough planning department, when a decision may take some six to eight weeks.

If your application is turned down, you can appeal to the next higher authority, and, in the case of a refusal by the county or borough planning departments, to the Ministry of Housing and Local Government. A decision or an appeal at this level can take several months.

Scheduled or listed buildings

You may find you have bought property that is scheduled as a work of architectural interest. If this is the case, you may be limited in what you can do to its external – and possibly even its internal – appearance. The planning department of your local authority will help you here.

Other restrictions

Some landlords operate their own planning and development controls over and above those of the planning authorities. This can occur when houses are sold on long lease and you should check before you finalize designs whether your landlords are in agreement with your proposals.

Relevant Acts and regulations

The following Acts all affect building work and should be consulted:
London Building Act 1930–1939 Constructional By-laws and Amendments (published by the Greater London Council);
The Building Regulations 1965 and Amendments (HMSO);
Public Health Act 1961 and Amendments (HMSO);
Town and Country Planning Act 1962 (HMSO).

The London Building Act is operative in the City of London and 12 Inner London Boroughs only, and is enforced by district surveyors appointed by the GLC to ensure that all constructional work is carried out in a workmanlike manner, the materials used are of a certain standard, that all by-laws are complied with and all operations are carried out to the satisfaction of the district surveyor. A fee is payable for this service.

The Building Regulations and Public Health Acts are operative in the rest of England and Wales. (Scotland has its own regulations of a similar nature.) All local councils have appointed building inspectors who ensure that all constructional works, drainage, sanitation, etc, comply with the regulations. No fee is payable for this service.

Under the Public Health Act the Inner London Councils have appointed public health officers whose duty is to ensure that all drainage construction, sanitation, materials, etc, meet their requirements and that all regulations are complied with. No fee is payable for this service.

The Town and Country Planning Act is mainly to ensure that building is regulated, kept to a fairly high standard and conforms to the surrounding buildings and/or countryside, to assist in maintaining the Green Belt, to prevent overcrowding and the erection of unsightly structures, and generally control development.

Regulations are in force regarding the supply of water, electricity and gas. The appropriate board should be consulted as required.

If you employ an architect, surveyor or reputable builder he will, of course, be conversant with the regulations and will advise as to what you may or may not do. Should you decide to employ casual labour or do the work yourself, do make sure that the work and materials conform to the regulations in force. Failure to do so may result in: (1) Appearance in a magistrate's court and a possible fine for failing to comply; (2) An order to demolish all unauthorized or unsatisfactory work.

You will find it a simple matter to call at your local town hall or district surveyor's office and ask to see the appropriate officer whom you will find most helpful – district surveyors, public health officers and building inspectors are not appointed to make things awkward but to ensure safe building.

Most minor alterations and repairs are permitted subject to inspection by a local officer. In the case of new work, application to your council and/or district surveyor will be necessary. For example: *New work*: erection of garage, lean-to, car-port, side or rear additional accommodation, room built in roof space, additional wc and/or bathroom – all of these will need drawings and planning permission; *Repairs and alterations*: removal of walls to enlarge rooms, dividing-up of rooms, any work to drains including renewal of wc pan, renewal of fireplace or tiled surround, and work to brickwork such as fitting a large window or enlarging a door opening. The local inspector/ surveyor will probably give permission subject to inspection. Remember that it is an offence to start on any works, as described here, before notifying the appropriate department or official.

Local authority grants

The new local authority grants are more generous and wide-ranging than many people realize. Even before you have actually bought your house, it is well worth getting a copy of the booklet *Money to Modernise Your Home* (from your local council offices) as this explains, in detail, what grants are available. If you are thinking of letting some of the space, you should also get the booklet *House Improvement and Rents*, which spells out what improvements you can make, even if you have statutory tenants, and what differences this can make to the rent you can charge them. There are two types of grant:

Standard Grants: for the provision of certain standard amenities in existing dwellings, which the council are obliged to pay if certain conditions are fulfilled.
Discretionary Grants: for thorough improvement of a house or flat to a high standard, or for providing dwellings by converting another type of building. The council may pay a part of the total cost at their discretion.

To apply for a grant you must be the freeholder or have at least five years' unexpired lease on your property. When you have decided – with your architect and/or builder – what improvements you want, you can ask advice from your local council on the best way to go about it. It is essential that you wait until the local council has approved your application before doing any new work. If, for instance, a roof urgently needs renewing before winter sets in, then your local authority may give you permission to go ahead, even before the grant is approved, but you should check first. The council may impose a time limit of not less than one year for getting the work done, but it is likely tha they would extend this period if necessary.

The grant is usually paid when the work is completed to the council's satisfaction, but sometimes, when the council considers it appropriate, discretionary grants may be paid by instalments during the course of the work. Not only can your local authority make you an outright grant, they may also give you a loan to cover your share of the cost of the work. If you are buying a house through a building society the local authority may be willing to extend your mortgage or lend you your share of the cost.

When you are taking on a house that is part-occupied, and the tenant will not consent to the improvements you want to make, your local council will advise you whether you can apply to the county court for an order empowering you to enter and carry out these works.

Standard Grants are made by local councils to help meet the cost of improving houses by providing any missing standard amenities for the first time. The standard amenities are:

(a) fixed bath or shower in a bathroom;
(b) wash-hand basin;
(c) sink;
(d) hot and cold water supply at a
    (i)   fixed bath or shower
    (ii) wash-hand basin
    (iii) sink;
(e) lavatory.

The amount of grant you can get is half the cost of the work, including professional fees. The normal maximum is £200 for providing all five improvements for the first time, and a lower maximum in other cases.

If the council are satisfied that it is not practical to provide a bath or shower without, say adding on or converting an outhouse, or to install a lavatory without connecting it to main drainage, they will allow you half the reasonable cost of this improvement, or something of this sort. The grant is then subject to an overall maximum of £450, instead of the normal £200.

To qualify for a Standard Grant the house must (a) have been in existence before 3rd October, 1961; (b) the standard amenities must be provided for the exclusive use of the occupants of the house; (c) the local council must be satisfied that after the work has been done the house will be in a good state of repair, disregarding internal decorative repair, having regard to its age, character and locality, and will in all other respects be fit for human habitation and likely to remain in that condition and available for use for at least fifteen years. Subject to these conditions, the council cannot refuse a valid application for a standard grant, unless the house is situated in a general improvement area, where a higher level of improvement will normally be the aim.

Discretionary Grants are made by local councils to help owners to bring old houses up to a good standard, or to provide new housing units by converting large houses and non-residential buildings. The council may pay up to one-half of the estimated cost of essential modernization, including professional fees. The maximum grant allowed is £1,000 for each flat or house improved. However, where flats are provided in a house or building of three or more storeys, the upper limit is £1,200 for each flat.

Generally, to qualify for a Discretionary Grant, a dwelling must after improvement:

(a) be in a good state of repair and substantially free from damp;
(b) have each room properly lighted and ventilated;
(c) have an adequate supply of wholesome water laid on inside the dwelling;
(d) be provided with efficient and adequate means of supplying hot water for domestic purposes;
(e) have an internal lavatory, if practicable – otherwise a readily-accessible outside lavatory;
(f) have a fixed bath or shower in a bathroom;
(g) be provided with a sink or sinks and with suitable arrangements for the disposal of waste water;
(h) have a proper drainage system;
(i) be provided in each room with adequate points for gas or electric lighting (where reasonably available);
(j) be provided with adequate facilities for heating;
(k) have satisfactory facilities for storing, preparing and cooking food;
(l) have proper provision for storing fuel (where required).

The Council may dispense with a requirement if satisfied that it cannot be complied with in a particular case.

Up to one-half of the approved amount of the discretionary grant may cover works of repair or replacement incidental to some other improvement or which the council feels necessary to make some other improvement fully effective. Although repairs and replacements by themselves do not qualify for a grant, the council may be prepared to make a loan to cover their cost. If the works turn out to be more expensive than you had first thought, the council may increase the grant they gave you.

If a standard grant has already been granted to the house, and you wish to make further improvements, the council may still give a discretionary grant to bring it up to a better standard.

How to read an architect's drawings

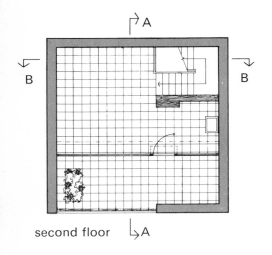

second floor

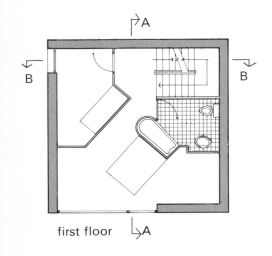

first floor

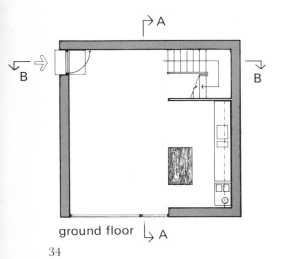

ground floor

Architects' drawings are usually thought to be more complicated than they really are and people are often convinced, even before they look at them, that they will be incomprehensible. Yet it is only by studying these floor plans and sections that the merits or faults in a building can be seen and its spatial character understood. Perspective drawings can be misleading and, at best, can only show a number of isolated viewpoints.

The plans themselves reveal only half the story. They show the areas of the various rooms, how the rooms are related and the position of things like cupboards, but they cannot tell more. It is the cross-section – in conjunction with the plans – which demonstrates how all the elements of the building are related to each other in three dimensions. This is especially so if there are any complexities in level, when it is often difficult to make sense of a plan without at least one section.

It is most important when you study drawings to know what information they are intended to give. For example, although it may be difficult for an untrained eye to gain much information from the 'working' drawings from which a building is built, it should be possible from a clear set of 'client's' drawings to get a precise idea of how the building works and how the spaces in it are related to one another.

Plans and sections are diagrammatic cuts made horizontally (in the case of plans) and vertically (in the case of sections) through the building to show what happens inside.

Where the cuts are taken depends very much on the building. Obviously, it is usually necessary to make a plan cut at every floor level, although, in certain cases, two different floor levels can be shown on the same drawing when they do not come one directly above the other. With sections, the choice is obviously more difficult to make, but they are usually taken at points which will show most details of the building.

The first thing to look for is where the cuts for the plans and sections are made. With plans, look to see how one fits above the other (it is always easier to begin with the lowest floor and work up). See how

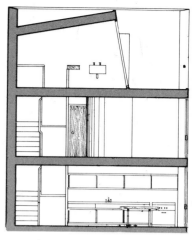

section A A

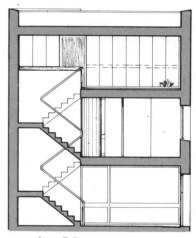

section B B

flights of stairs are linked. All staircases have directional arrows which show which flight rises to the next floor. One broken line, as shown on the ground floor plan, or two broken lines, as on the first floor plan, indicate that the horizontal plan cuts have been made at these points in the staircase.

When reading floor plans, take a mental walk through the building. Start at the entrance and move through the various rooms, then go up the stairs and do the same on each floor. A quarter-circle is used to show which way doors swing.

When reading sections, the first thing to do is to discover where the cut has been made and into which part of the house you are looking. This can be done by reference to the plans on which the section lines are marked by arrows to show in which direction you are facing. By continually comparing the sections with the plans, it is simple to build up a complete picture of the house.

To make plans and sections more readily understandable, the parts of the building through which the cut is made are always outlined with thicker lines or are blocked in, while the objects seen in the background are more finely drawn.

Other drawing terms you may come across are:

Elevation: drawings of the different sides of a building drawn to scale to show the exact size and relationship of the doors, windows and other features.

Axonometrics: geometrical drawings which give a three-dimensional, though somewhat unreal picture of a building. They are developed from the actual plan and all measurements on the horizontal planes (flat roofs and floors) and all vertical dimensions (walls) are accurate. Only the curves and diagonals on vertical planes are inaccurate.

Isometrics: a more realistic version of the building but, in order to do this, the basic plan has to be distorted with the result that diagonals and curves on both horizontal and vertical planes are inaccurate.

Perspectives: drawings of a building seen from an angle; three-dimensional views which correspond with what is seen by the eye.

The three plans (opposite) and two sections (above) of a three-storey house show the horizontal and vertical cuts through its floors. To illustrate the points involved, the floors vary considerably in layout and some of the shapes may seem unusual, but by studying the various parts of the building both in plan and section, it becomes possible to get a complete idea of the whole house

USING THE PLAN

The town house you are most likely to find is some variation of the standard terrace house with its front door to one side and two main rooms running front to back, plus a great variety of back extensions. Using the structure pretty much as it stands is clearly the least expensive way of taking over a house. But even if you don't want to make large-scale alterations, you can vastly improve the circulation and sense of space in a house simply by blocking up the odd door, opening up new ones, removing an unnecessary fireplace, or dropping the sill of a window leading into the garden to make a glazed door.

If you are prepared for the upheaval of knocking down walls, changing the position of staircases, or opening up areas of the ground floor to the basement, this can turn what seemed a boxy little house into something utterly different – a light airy space with long vistas and unexpected changes of level. This sense of space is, of course, partly illusory, although any changes that result in tightening the circulation will also provide more *usable* living space, making it easier to place furniture and so on.

Circulation is the word architects use to describe the links between rooms within a house and those between the house and the outside. These include paths, porches, entrance-halls, corridors, staircases and landings. Circulation is the key to successful planning; if it is compact and well-organized, maximum space will be gained for the rooms themselves. So, while you are deciding which room will be best for a study, or a dining-area, think how you will want to place furniture and how you will move around the house generally. Consider the position of doors: are they in the best place? Would it be more convenient if they were moved to another position, hung the other way, replaced by a sliding door or even blocked up entirely to give more wall space? At the same time, check whether fireplaces will be needed; if not, their surrounds can be stripped off, the hole blocked up and plastered over to give you 5 feet or so of useful wall-space. Sometimes, the chimney-breast can be removed completely or instead of blocking

Simple, but effective ways of opening up the room of a London terrace-house can be seen in this conversion by architect Bill Siddons. The cross beam which carries a track for spotlights replaced the original dividing wall between the first floor front and back rooms. The space has been further opened up by removing most of the wall that divided the narrow backroom from the staircase well. This too carries a track for lights. The existing window has been made wider and carried down to the ground which links the room with the garden despite its higher level. The original fireplaces and recesses have been blocked off and the surrounds stripped away to provide a continuous wall plane which unifies the space. Skirting radiators running along the base of this wall ensure a good spread of heat across the entire room

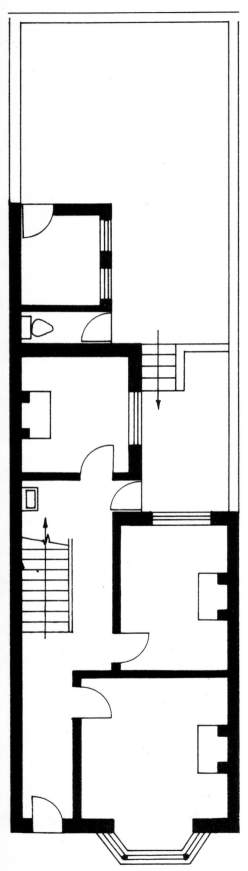

it up, you could open it into a recess reaching almost to the ceiling. Giving it an arched or flat head, it could then house shelves or be given doors to form a cupboard.

Don't let the house's present structure straight-jacket your imagination. Even the front door should be given careful thought. The space taken up by an entrance-hall in a semi-detached house, for example, might be put to far better use as a study or kitchen if the door is switched from the front to the side. If you are faced with a long narrow hall, glazed doors will break it up to make a heat-saving draught lobby. Or, provided it would suit the façade of the house, you could shorten the hall by recessing the front door to form a porch. Space-wasting staircases can often be replaced by more compact, better-sited ones, and space saved in the centre of the house exploited by mechanical ventilation to become bathrooms, cloakrooms and utility rooms.

With a deep, narrow house, it sometimes pays to move the staircase from the front or the back of the house, and set it across the middle. This opens the entire back of the house into one wide room with windows overlooking the back garden. Similarly, the same middle section of the house can be used to provide bathrooms with artificial light and ventilation.

Step-saving and space-saving apart, entrance-halls, stairs and landings can do a great deal to establish the mood of the house and deserve more attention than they usually receive. And as one moves through them rather than staying in them for long periods, they can take considerably more dramatic treatment than the rest of the house. To get light into the stairwell it is sometimes worth taking the solid panels out of doors and replacing them with clear glass to allow long shafts of light to fall through the house. This can be most attractive when one steps into the entrance-hall of what appeared to be a dark and gloomy house, to find light and sunshine pouring in from the garden beyond.

Perhaps the most obvious way of creating one generous space is to open front and back rooms – on any floor – into one. In the basement, it can be in the form of a large hatch opening between kitchen and dining-room; on the ground floor it can provide one large sitting-room; on the first floor you might link a sitting-room and a study, a

The plan on the left shows the ground floor of a typical mid-Victorian, non-basement terrace house. The rooms are small, the front bay-window, an Edwardian addition, and the outhouses eat into the space of the tiny back yard.

On the right the plan illustrates how the space can be remodelled while keeping basic alterations to a minimum. The two small rooms are opened up into one, which makes it possible to block the front room's door to the hall. A second, glazed door is added at the other end of the entrance hall so that it becomes a bedroom and a study or a bedroom and dressing/bathroom in this way. Opening up front and back rooms to make one can be done in a variety of ways. You can either maintain the sense of two linked but independent spaces, or try to achieve the sense of one large room. The first can be useful if you wish to use the two parts in slightly different ways. In my own house, I have blocked up the door that formerly led from my narrow front entrance-hall to the front room and have opened up the wall between that room and the one behind it, entering the combined space through the existing back room door which leads from the staircase lobby. The blocked-off door in the front part of the room allows for a much easier and generous seating arrangement. The back room acts clearly as an ante-room to it and contains walls of books and the desk I use for personal letters and family files. It is important to give a back room a specific purpose, otherwise it tends to be under-used. It could be a place to keep your piano, music, stereophonic equipment or to give formal dinner parties if you usually eat in the kitchen. Or it could make a study, perhaps for someone who has to work in the evenings but dislikes being cut off completely from the family.

Combining the two rooms in this way, rather than keeping them as two separate units, does allow for the possibility of a large space for parties and the pleasure of light penetrating from two different sides. The opening can be formed in several ways. One of the most elegant in a Georgian or Regency house is an elliptical arch, but sadly this isn't the easiest or cheapest thing to have done these days as it needs such careful setting out. A simple rectangular opening, with a $1\frac{1}{2}$-inch thick timber lining which has half-round edges projecting $\frac{3}{4}$-inch beyond the face of the plaster, in each room is a more practical solution. An opening of this sort can also take curtains or folding or sliding doors if you ever want to shut the rooms off from each other. If you want the two rooms to seem truly like one, the dividing wall needs to be cut back so that no projecting nib shows on either side and you will need to get advice on whether this is possible structurally.

Knocking down the dividing wall means that the weight of the wall and floor joists above, which almost invariably run front-to-back in town buildings, will have to be carried by something else, probably

self-contained space and effective draught trap. The front bay has been removed and replaced by a triple sash more appropriate to the period of the house. In the new double room the back fireplace is blocked off. The window in the back room has been replaced by french doors.

The chimney breast in the back kitchen has been removed, and by removing the outhouses it was possible to make a new kitchen window. Wide, shallow steps replace the narrow steep ones which lead up into the back garden, and a summerhouse is set along the back wall

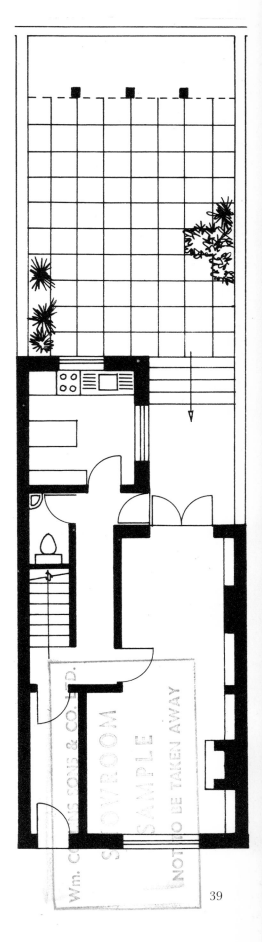

39

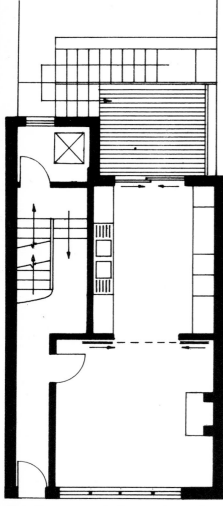

On the ground floor plan of a terrace house double doors link front and back rooms. The door from the hall to the back room is blanked off, and the space fitted as a kitchen. Glazed sliding doors open on to a terrace which has steps leading down to the garden. The front room can double as a dining-room or children's playroom. A boiler to heat the whole house is installed in the back extension

a concrete or steel beam. It is easiest to let this drop below the ceiling level but by doing so it tends, visually, to divide the space even where the wall has been totally removed, leaving no projecting nibs. If the span is not too wide (which will demand a deep beam), it may be possible to lose the beam in the thickness of the floor above, but this is a more disruptive undertaking.

It is often useful to open up the wall between two small children's bedrooms on an upper floor. Folding or sliding doors can give the rooms privacy when they are used as bedrooms, but opened up, they will provide generous playing space during the day.

With a small narrow terraced house, another way of gaining more space on the plan is to remove the wall between the back room and the staircase lobby. If this is done, the front room can remain self-contained – so that its existing door is left opening into the front entrance-hall. The front entrance-hall can then be given a glazed door to separate it from the newly opened up staircase lobby. This can be done most successfully when the back room is used as a dining-room with the kitchen in the back extension opening directly off it. With the dividing wall down, and the back room opened up into the staircase lobby, a far larger table can be comfortably accommodated. The staircase itself could remain open to the dining-room but, if you want more privacy, its balustrade could be removed and a partition wall built in its place. The front ground floor room could be used as a study, or as a room for an *au pair*, and the sitting-room could be on the first floor. By opening up the wall between the front entrance-hall and the front room a useful space for prams, tricycles and a play area for children on wet days can be created. One could knock down this front dividing wall equally successfully in a small house, so that the front room becomes a dining-room and the back room a kitchen. But it would be wise to leave enough of the dividing wall standing to make a small draught lobby at the front door. In the house designed by Stout & Litchfield, shown on the cover and on page 76, a wall was taken down in this way (as well as the central dividing wall) and this whole space is now used as a sitting-room. Some of the floor at the back is cut away to provide a gallery which overlooks the floor below. The vista now achieved gives a remarkable sense of space in what is in fact a fairly narrow house.

The degree of open-planning you want depends on the way the house is to be used. Unless a separate nursery is available, open-planning does pose considerable problems with very small children. It can be noisy and great care has to be taken that food smells are thoroughly absorbed and controlled at source. But, so long as there are adequate bolt-holes for those who want to work quietly or are likely to make a lot of noise, then opening up the structure can transform a 'mean' house into one with exciting and generous space.

To give longer vistas and to break up the rigidity of the existing structure, however, doesn't necessarily demand that whole walls have to come down. There are examples on pages 44 and 45 which show walls simply pierced, with narrow floor-to-ceiling strip openings, which give a sense of the space beyond without opening up the rooms completely. A lot of this sense of space and freedom is provided by the lack of doors which can act as barriers. Sometimes, one can get the best of both worlds – the freedom of open-planning with the privacy of self-contained rooms – by fitting floor-to-ceiling sliding panels or doors. This yields a more flexible solution – adaptable to the demands of the moment.

Another way of gaining space, and width in particular, is to fit mirrors from floor to ceiling and wall to wall. These double the existing sense of light and space. A tiny room will feel much less claustrophobic if one whole wall is mirrored. Even though there is no more space for your body to move around in, the wall still seems to be twice as far away.

The best position for a mirror is usually at right-angles to the main source of light, so that it can reflect sunshine, nearby plants and views of the garden generally. A mirror could back both recesses on either side of a chimney-breast in a small ground-floor room. Another obvious place to use the mirror as a space and light doubler is in long narrow entrance-halls where, of course, it has a practical function as well.

Dropping high window sills down to the ground to make glazed doors or a full-length window lets light flood across the floor itself, carrying the eye outside into the space beyond. This is even more effective where there is a balcony or light-reflecting terrace beyond. Another way of extending living space, both practically and visually, is to build on a greenhouse or conservatory. These can provide additional living space as well as an inviting green vista from the existing house. They could also include a temporary sandpit and be used as a play area for toddlers in bad weather. Or, more handsomely treated, it could provide a dining-room or a sitting-room for sunny winter afternoons.

If you decide to build a greenhouse, it is well worth making it take on double duty as a year-round living space. The quality of light can be modulated if it becomes too bright or too hot. Heating need not be a problem. There will always be some heat-loss from the house, which will help a little, and this can be supplemented by either radiators run from the central heating system or by some sort of independent electric heater which can be thermostatically controlled and turned up higher when the place is used. Probably the best treatment is background heat, because heat-loss with so much glass will inevitably be fairly great. However, double glazing units can do a great deal to offset this

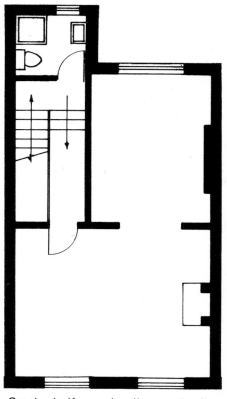

On the half-way landing to the first floor the cloakroom doubles as a shower-room for the ground and first floors. Front and back rooms are opened up to provide a large sitting-room with a study area at the back. The door from the landing to the back room has been blocked up, so has the fireplace

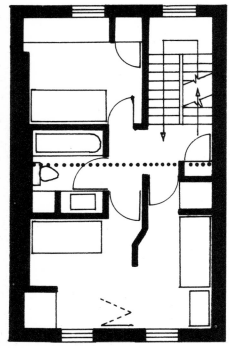

This upper-floor plan of a terrace house shows how it can be adapted to provide three bedrooms and a bathroom. Two of the bedrooms are divided by sliding, folding panels which can open them up into one sizeable room. The dividing wall (see dotted line) between the original front and back rooms has been removed and an internal bathroom set centrally between the two chimney breasts of these former rooms. The cranked wall between the two linked bedrooms allows for access to the rooms, yet sufficient width in the rooms themselves. All storage is built-in

and if you use the room a lot, it would certainly be worth installing them.

Where you have a flat roof extension and don't want to build other floors on top of it, you will probably find it can be reached simply by making a door from the half-landing nearest to it, as these back rooms usually are set halfway between the main floors of the house. There will probably be a window opening in the right position and it may be simply a question of dropping this to make a glazed door. If access to a flat roof is reasonably easy, this could be developed to provide the sort of greenhouse/conservatory I have been talking about, but at a higher level, the parapet forming a base for the framing and the glazing panels. As the joists supporting this flat roof won't be strong enough for it to be used as a floor, it would be unwise to load it with heavy pots. For such a project it would be worth getting professional advice to check this, or at least to employ a really reliable builder to carry out the work.

I have dealt mainly with ways of finding more floor space in this section, but there is a great deal to be said for knocking off such existing excrescences as bay windows or outhouses if they have been added since the house was originally built. Both early-Victorian town houses we have converted for ourselves had Edwardian bay windows added to the original structure. Each was in rather saggy condition and let water in. Visually they were clumsy and too large-scale for the façade, especially with a small, elegant round-headed door alongside them. In both cases, I replaced them with a triple sash which is one way of infilling the large opening left and which is in keeping with the original period of the house. Although you lose space, you do in fact gain a deeper penetration of light into a room when the projection of the bay is removed.

Again, it is often worth knocking down the crumbling outhouses at the back of the house and opening up the back wall of the main structure to light and air. Certainly you lose outside storage space but it is often better to allow this in the garden. Certainly, you are left with a better garden shape.

Two views of the living area in the upper, self-contained maisonette of a house owned and converted by architects Roy Stout and Patrick Litchfield. The first floor is given over to a large, freely-planned living area opening onto a balcony at the front of the house. To open up the space the central load-bearing wall was replaced with two steel beams concealed by lowered ceilings. The small study at the back of the living area can be shut off by folding doors, or left open as a visual extension of that space. The kitchen and dining area are on a half level down; at this point the rooms are open to the staircase so that from the front of the living area it is possible to appreciate the full depth of the house on the two adjacent split levels. A sense of spaciousness and continuity is achieved by the consistent use of a few materials

In his own house in Chalk Farm architect Christopher Todd Hunter has experimented with a way of opening up the wall between the first floor front and back rooms of a terrace house. He has pierced the wall with two tall, narrow strips which allow for a flow of space and light between the two rooms and at the same time provide efficient screening to define the individual volume and activity of each room.

The wider rooms, running across the house, are used as a sitting-room and heated by a handsome Pither stove. The smaller back room, overlooking the garden, serves as the dining — kitchen area; the floor-to-ceiling cupboards, designed by the architect, provide ample storage space while giving the effect of an elegantly textured wall. The original floorboards were sanded and walls and woodwork are painted white

The dividing wall between the ground-floor front and back rooms of this Early Victorian house was taken out to make a through living-room/study in a conversion by architect John Prizeman. The newly-created space was kept intentionally simple with walls and ceiling areas uncluttered by mouldings or light fittings. The smooth modern lines of the room are a perfect foil for the handsome original windows at either end. Two recesses remain in the room — one contains a built-in bookshelf unit, the other provides space for a sofa. The plain haircord carpet throughout further emphasizes the simplicity of the treatment. The bold screen prints are the work of the owner, illustrator David Gentleman

Architect Anthony Cloughley's Regency house in Chester Row offered him the scope and space to create the kind of place he wanted to live in. The L-shaped drawing-room shown here was made by opening up the two first-floor rooms and benefits from the combination of two windows at the front and the one overlooking the tiny paved garden at the back, which between them give a great deal of light. At night the room is lit by recessed ceiling spotlights while, in contrast, areas of light are spread upward by carefully positioned floor spotlights. The decoration is the work of Baron Alessandro Albrizzi who has made a great play of textures in the rooms. The soft beige felt of the drawing-room wall, for instance, makes an unusually successful background for Mr Cloughley's collection of modern pictures and kinetic art. Its softness contrasts well with the roughness of the oatmeal tweed-covered sofas, the glass tables, modern whatnots and the steel table and furniture frames. Apart from the canvas backed Christiansen Chairs, all the rest of the furniture was designed by Albrizzi. This is a fine example of the right use of a patterned carpet as all the other decorative elements provide only textural contrast

Composer Richard Rodney Bennet's house in Canonbury was generously enriched with moulded ceilings and elaborate ceiling roses, so that when he decided to open up two rooms to make one large sitting-room his concern was to preserve the period feeling. Instead of leaving a small nib of wall he used handsome Corinthian columns to carry the beam that takes the load of the wall and floors above. The ceiling rose was left as a decorative element in its own right. Although the fireplaces were removed from both rooms, the placing of the large pieces of furniture maintains the room's balance. Ceiling lights have been dispensed with, spots flood light onto the pictures, while table lamps spread more light at a lower level

Architect Tom Manning removed the rear wall of this house in Twickenham to open up the kitchen (now an internal room) to the new glass-walled, dining-room extension (shown on this page). A side door from the dining-room leads into the splendid conservatory (opposite). This exemplifies one of the happiest ways of achieving a spread of horizontal space; neither house nor garden loses, in fact both gain considerably, and an enchanting inside/outside area is created which makes boundaries hard to define. Here the detailing contributes enormously: the boarded ceiling, sturdy timber framing of the windows and glazed panels, large-scale tiles, and unplastered brickwork, act as splendid foils for the forms of interesting objects and luxuriant plants which provide the only enrichment

Two examples showing different ways of using a glazed extension to provide additional living space.

London decorator Lila Bailoni added the glass-walled room (shown opposite and right, above) to her small ground-floor flat in Belgravia. Basically an off-the-peg prefabricated extension, it was painted as simulated wood by decorator James Smart, with the window glazing outlined in blue, a touch that lifts the result out of its 20th-century origins. The 'pavilion' makes a sunny breakfast room and by night an exotic dining-room. A roller blind set at the top of the sloping roof acts as protection from over-fierce sun.

Architect Ivor Smith's ingenious extension, incorporating a kitchen with bedroom over it, is shown right, below. The floor of the bedroom is on a level with the top frame of the vertical window but is set back to allow extra light to flood into the kitchen from the sloping middle section of glazing. The upper sloping section of glazing belongs to the bedroom

Here again a glass-covered loggia extension is used to open up a room space, visually and practically — this time in architect Max Clendinning's conversion of a London mews house. The transition from the sitting-room, through the newly opened-up loggia, into the small open courtyard beyond provides the sort of progression of spaces which transforms a maze of rooms into an interior full of surprises and enchanting vistas. In addition the new extension floods light into the main sitting-room. The spaciousness of the sitting-room is further enhanced by the mirror-like finish of the walls.

The skilful planting of a glass extension or conservatory can further help to open up the inside of the house by providing an inviting green vista to draw the eye out to the space beyond. Well-stocked plant benches and hanging baskets, such as those shown left, below, also offer town-house dwellers the delight of green growing things all the year round

This magnificent space started life as part of a Hampstead coach house. The entrance to the house (above) is a paradoxical prelude to the spaciousness of the interior. The conversion, devised by industrial architect Norman Foster, was deceptively simple: two long concrete-block walls were built parallel to the major elevations of the coach house, a flat industrial decked roof was added over the projected living area and a sloping glazed roof over the dining area. The metal beams, left exposed and finished with aluminium paint, support the first floor. The sloping roof was pitched up to the eaves of the old house so that the wall below could be knocked out — transforming a cramped upstairs room into a spacious gallery. No doors interrupt the flow of space and aluminium-framed shop doors and windows fill the open ends. A visual contrast to the deliberate austerity and ruggedness of the shell is provided in the use of soft shaggy carpets, vast sofas and touches of brilliant colour

Walls, even structural ones, can be removed, and beams inserted to carry the loads, in order to open box-like rooms into flowing space. The conversions here show how this was done with great effect in two typical terrace houses.

Architect John Benson opened up the top floor of his three-storey 1830's London terrace house (opposite, above) into a living-room, to take advantage of the views and all available sunlight. It is often easier to take out walls in a top floor than elsewhere, and as no staircase runs up through this part of the house the living-room can occupy the full floor area. The existing ceiling was stripped out leaving, as a result, ten-foot high walls, far more appropriate in scale to so large an area. Pine boarding has been used for the new ceiling, which follows the contours of the roof. The dining-room and kitchen (opposite, below) are at a half level lower, housed in a two-storey extension, already existing at the back of the house. The positioning of these rooms extends diagonally the apparent size of the living area while keeping the rooms' different functions separate. There is the additional advantage that cooking can be done without isolation from family and guests.

Most walls have been removed from the dining and kitchen area of the maisonette conversion by architects Stout and Litchfield shown above. Floor-to-ceiling doors can, when necessary, shut off the staircase and although the kitchen is open to the dining-room, so that the person cooking is not isolated from guests and family, the pass-through hatch is designed to mask the clutter of food preparation. The suspended pine ceiling conceals the new structural beams and gives a feeling of continuity to the whole area

A problem common to extensions is that they can seriously cut off the light from the room to which they are attached. In the serene-looking sitting-room, opposite, (part of an extension designed by architects Desbrow and Hille), the problem is solved by fitting sliding glass doors from floor-to-ceiling and wall-to-wall on the garden side, and a long glazed panel in the roof which floods down light onto the extension's back wall. A venetian blind shuts this off at night and cuts out glare during the day. Although the space is so simply treated, the natural materials — the boarded floors and ceiling, unplastered brickwork, and long chunky marble bench/shelf — provide not only texture and colour but an attractive foil to the planting outside.

The extension room above, designed by architect John Winter, again shows the use of a glass wall and a long skylight to gain light penetration. Here these are reinforced by two long narrow side windows which make the room seem wider

Architect Trevor Dannatt used the land at the side of his Early Victorian house in Islington to extend his living space sideways, by adding a garage with study over. The extension is built in second-stock brick which blends with the walls of the existing house. The original side porch provided the regulating line below which the new extension has been developed, which meant that ceiling heights had to be kept to a minimum. By accepting this line and providing a heavy capping to the new work, the completely modern treatment was made to relate to the formal classicism of the porch and window details. The side entrance to the back of the house is now through the garage which is fitted with a specially designed door incorporating a separate standard-width door for tradesmen. Access to the study (opposite, above) is from the front entrance porch, through a narrow door built in an original window opening (opposite, below right). The study is designed to face the back garden; the glazed area provides a visual link while some steel steps (shown left, below) provide the actual link with the garden. The flank wall of the house is preserved and the fine old brickwork has been incorporated in the new room as an attractive decorative feature (opposite, below left)

Although it appears architecturally modest this extension (left, below), in London NW3, by architect Keith Manners, conceals a richly complex internal space providing a sitting-room, working area, a gallery-bedroom and small kitchen and bathroom. It started life as a single-storey brick extension which had been used as a sculptor's studio. By building the walls up a little and

giving it a pitched roof it was possible to incorporate galleries to increase the available floor space, as well as providing long diagonal vistas. The structural treatment is of the simplest kind and is unashamedly exposed, defining and framing the interior spaces. The simplicity of the framing provides a sturdy foil for the rich shapes and textures of the owner's furnishings

The design of this unusual extension to the basement and ground floor levels of a four-storey Victorian terrace house, by architect John Winter, took into account a number of considerations, among them being an irregularly-shaped site, neighbours' ancient rights of light and, not least, a view of the canal. The ground floor dining area (opposite) is the full height of the extension with a completely glazed wall broken only by the terrace on the upper level; both levels afford fine views across the grass to the canal. The kitchen, under the gallery, adjoins the dining-room; above it is the study-gallery (left, below) with a small spare bedroom behind. The study, with built-in teak worktop, overlooks the dining area and opens on to the upper-level terrace

USING THE SECTION

The points covered in this chapter will be of particular use to people who live in some variation of the standard terraced house. The usual problem with these houses seems to be that one is living on a number of shelves, the only inter-communication being exhausting flights of steps.

Your first object, then, needs to be to rationalize the way you propose to live in the house so that you aren't forever running up and down stairs. The way you do this will, of course, depend on the way you like to live and the character of your household, but you should aim to group linked activities to as few floors as possible.

Children's rooms should be linked together, whether they are in the basement or at the top of the house. First floor sitting-rooms are extremely pleasant in many ways, particularly if they go right across the front of the house and are linked with the back room to have sun all day long, but, unless you have someone in the house who opens the front door for you, it does mean that either the room will get used considerably less than it might during the day, or you will be endlessly running down and up stairs.

As I work at home I have resolved the different levels of my house in the following way. The house, as we found it, had three floors and a basement, which was no more than a coal-hole and a store, with a back extension on two floors only. The problem was that it hadn't really enough rooms for all our activities, so, out of the existing shell, with limited additions, we had to find some additional space.

American designer Anne Hartman remodelled the inside of this tiny, two-storey terrace house to achieve the greatest amount of space. To do this she created a great central well out of an unwanted third-floor centre bedroom, onto which all the rooms now open and which is flooded with natural light from a pitched skylight above. From the upper bedroom floor one looks across to the master-bedroom at the front of the house and downwards into the dining area at the bottom of the shelf-lined wall; further through, and open to it, is the sitting-room

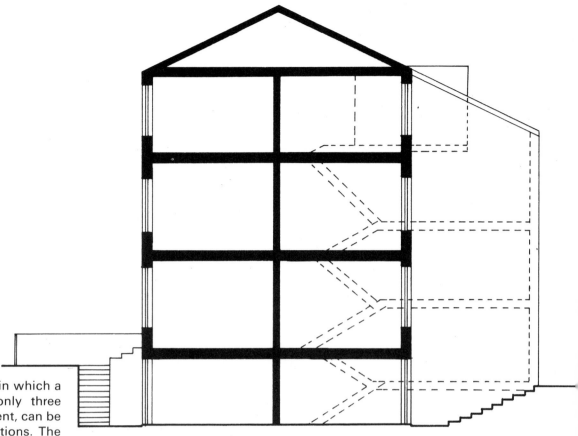

The section shows ways in which a house, with originally only three living floors and a basement, can be extended in several directions. The basement can be opened up to provide another living floor, with areas at the back and front giving access to the back and front garden. The central dividing wall between the two main rooms on any floor can be removed when one really big room is wanted. The dotted lines show how a back extension can be added beyond the staircase-well using the half-level landing of the stairs to provide access. Where the extension rises to the full height of the house, the main roof can be carried down over it and so relate it better to the existing structure. A dormer window can then give sufficient headroom and light to tuck an extra small room in at the very top

The first step was to give the basement a usable floor by opening up the front area and the steps at the back leading into the small garden. We then converted the basement into a kitchen, workshop/ utility room and dining-room at the back, a room sturdy enough in character to double as a play-room so that small children either there or in the garden beyond could be supervised. The original kitchen was halfway between the basement and the ground floor sitting-room and this seemed the best place for my work-room. Men can tuck a study away at the top of the house and block their ears to counter noise from below, but few women, unless they have a Mary Poppins, can switch off from their domestic life so completely. This does mean that, although my study is in the thick of things, I do have the bonus of working in a room that opens directly into a sunny garden, and during the day I seldom have to go up or down more than half a flight of stairs.

The bedrooms are on the two upper floors. My small son's room and the room for an *au pair* are at the very top and share a newly-made bathroom. We added two floors onto the existing two-storey back extension. These are accessible by the half-landings of the staircase.

The other bathroom has remained in its original position over what is now my study. Here we have simply re-planned and replaced the fittings. The lavatory was formerly in a separate compartment, but by putting it in the bathroom itself I have been able to adapt its old compartment to make a small laundry and cleaning recess, opening directly off the landing.

Apart from the flat roof over the bathroom which was in very poor condition, the extension was a pretty substantial structure, with reliable foundations, so we applied for permission to add on another two floors. Immediately above the bathroom we made a small study for my husband and, half over this and half over the top of the stairwell under the sloping roof, I tucked the second bathroom.

With an old building, you will always produce a far better result architecturally, if you can exploit the existing structure in your search for more space. You will also reduce maintenance and building costs by keeping under the same area of roof and avoid the need to excavate new foundations. Land is so valuable in cities, and a garden, however small, is such a pleasure in an urban environment, that it is worth trying very hard to avoid building out over it. Before building out sideways, first try to make better use of basements, your attics and roof spaces, or build on top of what extensions you have already – ie exploit the section.

Soundly-built back extensions frequently offer opportunities for building additional floors. The appearance of the back of the house is often improved when this is done and the main roof of the house is brought down over the top new room. Back extensions are usually on one or two floors only, and built of a different kind of brick. Carrying them to the full height of the house, under an extension of the main roof, does help to tie them in as an integral part of the building, especially if you decide to paint the brick work and thus unify the colour as well.

You won't always get permission to build on in this way, as the original structure may not be adequate to carry more floors, in which case it is worth thinking along the lines of a greenhouse/conservatory extension. This would impose much less load on the existing structure and would help to marry the extension to the original building in a more satisfactory way than by using the existing roof. There may not be a large enough area of light in the well left alongside the extension to satisfy building regulations, but this can be circumvented if you convert the turn rooms (which overlook it) into kitchens, bathroom/ utility rooms, etc – any room, that is, which is not technically 'habitable' in the way that bedrooms or living-rooms are. Another means of getting over this difficulty is to open up the wall between the front and back rooms, so that the overall space has ventilation from both the front and back of the house.

An interesting way of exploiting the section is to use the space provided by the very high ceilinged rooms sometimes found on the ground and the first floors, by forming a gallery. So long as you have a minimum headroom of 14 feet, 6 inches, a gallery is a possibility. Galleries can be useful in a great variety of rooms. In a sitting-room, for example, they can provide more accessible storage space for books, a place to have your desk or to keep hobby equipment out of the main area of activity. As the examples show, galleries can be valuable means of modulating the space of very large rooms by introducing a strong horizontal element. They certainly make it easier to relate the low lines of modern furniture to such very high ceilings and tall windows. And a lower ceiling over the fireplace area or the corner where you eat can produce an intimate ambiance in contrast to the soaring space of the rest of the room.

Where rooms are to be used as bed-sitting-rooms for children, or even as completely self-contained living units, sleeping galleries can be an invaluable way of providing half as much floor space again, with the added advantage of keeping the clutter of sleeping and dressing well out of the way.

There are all sorts of permutations, particularly if you are lucky enough to have found yourself a warehouse, a small factory or a shop to convert. Depending on the space you can allow for the gallery, you could perhaps fit a kitchen below and an artificially-ventilated bathroom on top. Where there is more room, the kitchen and bathroom could go below with a sleeping area above or perhaps a kitchen and eating area below, and the bathroom and sleeping area above. Where ceiling height doesn't allow enough height for both levels to be used for living on, the lower one could provide valuable storage space, some 4 feet high, to take trunks, suitcases and out-of-season sports gear.

The design of the balustrade will be influenced by the way you intend to use the gallery. For a gallery that is used for sleeping, a solid one might be more suitable. In a gallery which forms an integral part of a sitting-room, where the visual link of the two levels would be important, a lighter, open one would probably be preferable. A point to remember with balustrades is that they should be child-proof – you may have no children of your own but you can be sure your friends' children will make straight for it. Framing should be close enough to prevent a crawling infant pitching headfirst over the edge. Spiral stairs to the gallery will take up the least space. If you can find a cast-iron one being ripped out of an old building, it will be worth grabbing, even if it seems expensive. A new one will probably cost as much and may not be so pretty. Style Fitted Furniture of 245 Sutton Road, Southend-on-Sea, Essex SS2 5PE, sell handsome spiral stairs off-the-peg. They make two sizes; a standard stair of 6 feet 7 inches diameter, which would be useful where the main stair of the house is being

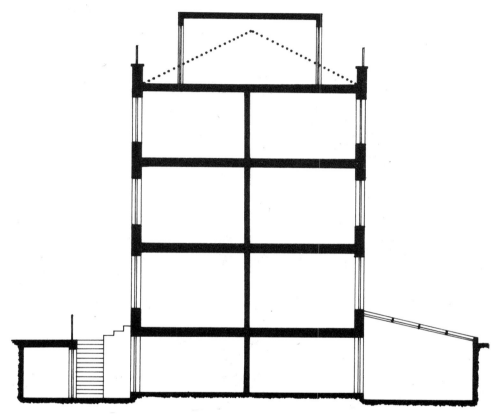

Basements and attics provide the greatest possibilities for extending the space of a house. The section gives one idea that can be used to open up an attic, another to extend the area of a basement. (For further ideas see sections on Attics and Basements.)

The new top floor can be built centrally in the old roof space leaving a narrow balcony at the back and front of the house which can be connected to the new room by glazed, sliding doors. The balcony at the front will ensure that the line of the parapet continues to link through with its neighbours and that the additional floor will be largely masked from the front, thus preserving the uniformity of a terrace.

The basement space can be extended by giving a glass roof to the back basement area. The back room wall onto it can then be opened up and fitted with glazed, sliding-doors; the newly-created space would make an ideal conservatory. At the front the vaults under the road can be opened up to the area and made into small grottos to make a visual extension of the space from the front basement room

replaced to make more space. Their 'compact' stair which is 5 feet 6 inches in diameter would be more appropriate for a gallery.

Another way of dealing with excessively high ceilings it to lower them, and this is certainly worth considering for internal bathrooms where a space 6 feet by 6 feet with a ceiling 12 feet high would feel about right. Dropping a ceiling does allow you to fit in pipes, possibly tanks, and a ventilation extraction duct above. Such a space can also be exploited by making high-level cupboards which open into the rooms on either side providing useful storage space for trunks and suitcases and other things that are used only occasionally. They are certainly much more accessible than they would be if stowed away in a loft.

Further means of making use of a ceiling which is high, but not high enough for a gallery, is to build storage cupboards at a high level. Given sliding doors, they can be absorbed into the general wall treatment.

The ground floor and basement of a four-storey London terrace house was converted by architects Stout and Litchfield into a maisonette. (For other views see the front and back cover.) Part of the existing ground floor has been cut away, leaving an eighteen-foot high void which transforms the original dark basement into a sunny living-room. By cutting away the floors and also removing parts of walls, horizontal and vertical spaces have been made to interrelate, breaking up the formality of the old box-like rooms. A view looking down into the living area from the ground-floor dining-kitchen gallery is shown above; the spaciousness is further enhanced by the small patio, with its shade-loving shrubs, which can be floodlit and used for outdoor dining in the summer. In the main area (right), the handsome, stainless steel Pither provides a focus of sculptural quality as well as warmth

In high-ceiling rooms galleries can be used as a means of getting more living space out of the same volume — often with striking effect.

In reorganizing the living space of his period house, off Boulevard Saint-Germain in Paris (shown above), interior decorator Kim Moltzer supported a sleeping-gallery on a deceptively light-weight structure of shelves and stairs.

Designers Paul Lester Wiener and Ala Damaz gutted an old town house and opened up a gallery above the library for use as a dining-room (opposite). The remarkably simple architectural treatment makes a successful foil for the splendidly rich furniture and *objets d'art*

The major conversion of this London mews house was undertaken by the owner, designer Alan Fletcher, with the help of a skilled carpenter. The first and attic floors were stripped out and partly replaced by gallery areas. The contours of the roof were lined throughout with tongued-and-grooved boarding and the galleries constructed out of timber beams which are left exposed. The ground-floor is now an enormous living space — the heart of the house — that spreads across the entire area (opposite). The one-time stable entrance that opened on to the mews is replaced by the floor-to-ceiling window and glazed door which allow light to penetrate into the space. The spiral staircase and balustrade, which lead to the studio gallery immediately over the sitting area, came from a demolished town hall. Above the dining area of the main living space, at the back of the house, are two galleries, shown on the right: the lower one accommodates the main bedroom (right, below) with a small bathroom and child's bedroom behind; the gallery under the eaves provides a storage area with a spare bedroom behind. The kitchen is at the back of the dining area

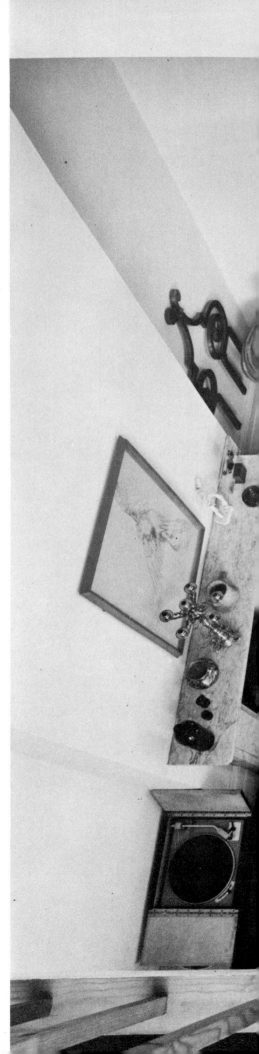

The picture opposite shows the view from the gallery that architect Bill Siddons created by opening up the ceiling of the ground-floor back room of his house in Fulham. This conversion achieves a double-height sitting-room which has high-level light spilling down into it from above. An eliptical arch was made to link this room with the one at the front of the house which doubles as a study and extra living space. Although all the original features have been retained — the panelled doors, handsome fireplace, moulded architraves and shutters to the windows — the house has a cool uncluttered modern look. Bedrooms open off the gallery; kitchen and dining-room are in the basement

This conversion by architects Stout and Litchfield illustrates an effective method of breaking through the rigid wall and floor system of a typical terrace house. By partially cutting away the back-room floors, and building galleries at half-landing levels, a series of diagonal vistas has been created. The picture, left, above, shows the view after entering the house from the small entrance lobby which is all that remains of the original long, narrow entrance hall on the ground floor. With the wall which originally divided the front and back rooms removed, the sitting-room now extends back as far as the chimney breast of the back room. Stairs lead down to the half-landing, (left, below): a further half flight leads down to the dining-room in the basement (opposite). The gallery above the far end of the dining-room is the same half-landing pictured left. The kitchen, a self-contained room at the front of the basement, has an effective extractor system to trap food smells at source — essential with this type of vertical open-planning. Bedrooms are on the two upper floors, on each of which an internal bathroom has been slotted into the middle of the house

Architects Geoffrey and June Hol-royd converted a seventeenth-century mansion in Blackheath to suit their family requirements. The whole of the immense ground floor of the building was made into one large apartment — 25 feet square and 14 feet high — adapted to cover a multiplicity of interests. Although the architects did not want to use the room for its original function, for dining and entertaining in the grand manner, they were determined to preserve its individuality and style. A gallery of steel decking was constructed, supported on a ten-inch by six-inch steel beam set into the existing brick piers. The decking, in two-inch wide sections, is supported between a three-inch square angle bolted to the walls, and a steel plate hung by long bolts from the flange of the beam. A half-inch ply facing encloses the steel beam, but the corrugated steel decking is exposed. Columbian pine stairs lead to the gallery bedroom (right, above). Sliding panels of hardboard-faced polystyrene, with black wood edges, conceal storage

One of the covetable Boston water-front buildings, shown here, was converted by its owner, architect Gerald Cugini. Three of the four floors of the building he designed for commercial use; he then set about raising the roof to create what is virtually a triplex residence for himself. The pitched roof is pierced by vast skylights that fill the whole space with natural light. On the bottom level is the combined music and living-room, main bedroom and study. The height of the living-room rises through the three full floors of the apartment, although the gallery dining-room (opposite) suspended within this space makes possible an intimately-scaled conversation area below. This is shown above. The dining-room is connected by a bridge (right) to the kitchen. Above, on the top gallery, are two guest bedrooms, a bathroom and a sitting area

THE BASEMENT

Your basement may well earn you an income as a self-contained flat, provide a room for living-in help, absorb the noise of children and hobbies, house the bulk of boilers and washing equipment, and even garage your car. The basement of my own Oxford house began life as a coal-hole and a dimly-lit store; it now provides a sizable kitchen, a utility/workshop and a dining-room with french doors which lead up steps to the garden. Happily, building societies are no longer prejudiced against basements when giving mortgages, as there are now so many effective ways of dealing with the problems of damp and poor ventilation.

Building regulations will govern the uses to which you can put your basement, but it may need only the right equipment and decoration or small structural alteration, to convert it into useful living space. Often, basements not eligible for conversion into proper 'living-rooms' can easily be made sufficiently dry and well ventilated for use as laundries, drying rooms, workshops and games-rooms, and to provide accessible storage space for bulk-buying (deep-freeze, jams, wines, etc).

If you are not using an architect, you should check before going too far with your plans that, when the basement is put to its proposed new use, it will comply with the appropriate building regulations. As a guide, in London, where conditions are most exacting, the Public Health Act (London 1936), Section 132 sets out minimum room heights, fixed and openable window areas, ceiling levels relative to pavement or ground level, area sizes, rules for external access and standards for building construction. The term 'underground room' covers any room with its floor level more than 3 feet below the adjoin-

Architect John Prizeman opened up the basement of the Early Victorian house in Regent's Park, shown opposite, with wall-to-wall glazed windows and doors at both ends, allowing more light to penetrate into the newly-created living floor. A ramp from the pavement, giving easy access to perambulators, leads into the area at the front of the house; the whitewashed walls reflect light into the basement room

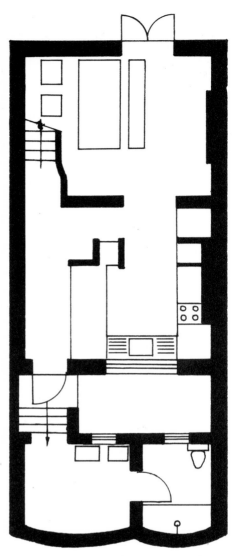

This basement plan shows how internal walls can either be opened up or removed entirely to make a linked dining-room and kitchen. In addition the vaults under the road can be developed to provide extra space, perhaps for a utility room and extra bathroom. A four-foot wide opening in the wall between the front and back rooms makes access between them easy, and allows space and light to flow through. The back window has been replaced by french doors leading into the garden, and the staircase well removed completely to enlarge the dining-room. The wall between the kitchen and area access lobby has been taken down and replaced by a work-top. The position of the hob will allow an extractor hood over it to exploit the existing flue

ing pavement or ground. The rest of England and Wales, although not Scotland (which has its own), is covered by the Building Regulations 1965, and these make reasonably similar demands. Of course, if you take over a basement which, although not conforming to these standards, is currently in use as living space, you will be permitted to continue to use it in this way unless you are applying for a discretionary grant when conditions may be made. Clearly, it is in your own interest and will add to the value of the property if you improve its amenities as much as possible.

It probably helps to consider what possibilities exist for improving basements, generally, before you determine finally what would be the best use for yours. The main problems are usually light, ventilation, damp and insufficient headroom. It may well be possible to increase the source of light sufficiently by widening or dropping the existing windows where an area already exists. Entrance doors can be glazed, and Georgian wired polished plate glass should give you sufficient security against burglars.

The most effective way to open up a basement to more light is to cut the earth away from the basement wall, and then to widen and drop the window sill down to floor level. Wide, shallow steps leading up into the garden at the back of the house give a very shallow penetrating angle of light and prevent the basement from being claustrophobic. Cutting away at the front of the house will depend on how much space there is between your front wall and the pavement. The larger the area, the more light can penetrate but, inevitably, the more costly the operation. If you pave areas with light-coloured slabs and paint walls white, the amount of light entering the basement both directly from the sky and indirectly from the area will be increased enormously.

Wherever you need obscured glass for privacy or to block an ugly view, you can use prismatic glass, with attractive narrow ribbing, which 'bends' light from the sky horizontally into the room. Use large mirrors indoors to reflect back the light that does penetrate. Next to mirrors, white surfaces are the most reflective, so where it is practical use white for walls, ceilings and paintwork. Yellows come next and bring a feeling of sunshine as well as light. These are followed by pale greens, blues and beiges or greys and these are a good choice for floors, although white of course is best of all and is particularly helpful when ceilings are low. Plain white floors do show dirt easily, but a travertine finish helps to disguise marking effectively. To bring light into the dark middle part of a deep, through basement, use screened daylight fluorescent tubes. They blend more sympathetically with natural daylight than tungsten bulbs. There is one firm, Illuminated Ceilings, which uses fluorescent tubes behind a translucent panel which gives a useful spread of light over the entire room, but one needs sufficient floor-to-ceiling height to accommodate this. Opening up the partition wall between front and back rooms in basements, so that light penetrates from both sides, helps to create longer vistas and a feeling of more light, and is well worth doing when the use of the rooms permits it.

Another problem in basements is insufficient headroom. It is often possible to get around this by ripping up the existing floor and excavating another 6 inches or so. This gives you a good opportunity at the same time to make a thoroughly waterproof floor. In dropping the floor, one has to ensure that the base of the walls and the foundations of the front and back party walls are still given sufficient support. By thickening the perimeter walls at their base and using these as plinths for cupboards or bench seating, one can often get over this problem. Where dropping the floor is impossible and the ground floor room has a high ceiling, it might well be possible to raise its floor by lifting floorboards and floor joists and so give at least 6 inches to the floor below. This sounds a pretty disruptive job but in fact could be carried out easily. The front hall could contain any steps required to accommodate the new changes from outside to inside.

If you can afford to lose the space on the ground floor, the most dramatic way of getting more light and headroom is to open up the basement ceiling, either partially or completely, in the back room. As a result, the room on the ground floor relates as a gallery to the room below.

Basements will be damp if they are not protected by a damp-proof membrane from moisture in the earth beneath the floor and surrounding the walls. Old houses rarely have any form of damp-proofing and even if they do this may well have broken down. You may find a sound boarded floor with no hint of damp or dry rot, but more probably you will find it failing, particularly at the edges. When taking over a house, especially if you are carrying out a major conversion, it is worth using the opportunity to put down a more reliable dry floor. There should be a damp-proof membrane over the entire floor area. This will mean lifting the boards or slabs already there, laying a concrete floor slab and damp-proof membrane, plus screed as a base for some insulating floor finish, such as cork, foam-backed lino or vinyl.

Where a washable floor isn't necessary, foam-backed carpet will help to give insulation against cold. Where depth will allow, try to include a layer of insulation such as glass quilt or 1-inch thick rigid polystyrene foam between the floor slab and the screed and so provide additional insulation.

Quarry tiles and other hard floors make practical and handsome floors for basements. I found some old red quarries in my basement which were fit to keep and brushed them with one of the new polyurethane damp-proofers designed to seal off rising damp. These are quite colourless but give a slight sheen to the material they are used on. I chose this means of damp-proofing because, although I had little evidence of rising damp, I was pretty sure from the age of the floor that there was no damp-proof membrane. It wasn't practical to have the floor up, as the existing drains, which were in excellent condition, ran only an inch or so beneath the floor surface.

If you find yourself with a concrete floor in reasonably good condition, but you are not certain that there is a damp-proof membrane somewhere beneath it, you can treat it with one of the water-proof seals mentioned above, simply finishing it with a levelling screed between $\frac{1}{16}$- and $\frac{1}{8}$-inch thick, where head-room is limited, or you can give it either a bituminous or polythene membrane and top it with $1\frac{1}{2}$ - to 2-inch screed where you have the head-room.

There are several ways in which you can treat damp walls, and many local councils are prepared to give grants towards damp-proofing basements. Rentokil's electricosmotic system is very reliable, and the MDC now provide a similar service as well. British Knapen Gallwey, Actane, and Peter Cox have all proved themselves over the years, and your nearest Building Centre will provide pamphlets and addresses. (See also the chapter, *Dealing with the structure*.) While drying out is taking place, it may be worth stripping the crumbling plaster off the walls, simply wirebrushing the brick or stone you find behind and painting the resulting surface with an old-fashioned distemper or water paint which will allow the walls to breathe. Where a plastered surface is wanted, or where for some reason it is difficult to dry out the wall, Newtonite, a vertically corrugated bituminous felt, makes a very satisfactory damp-proof skin. The vertical corrugations help ventilate the wall itself and provide a good key for plaster. Damp internals walls should never be waterproofed in this way as the damp would be sealed in and the fabric would decay. For such walls you must select a system which will check the damp at the bottom of the wall.

Treating damp, however, is a specialized business, and I can only suggest lines to follow up. This is why it is worth going to a reputable firm which will give you a long-term guarantee rather than rely on the little builder around the corner.

Poor ventilation, of course, is often the cause of dampness, dry rot and condensation in basements. To overcome this, plan for cross-currents and through draughts. Fit openable fan-lights or louvres over or in the panels of doors, and electric extractor-fans in bathrooms and kitchens and utility rooms. If one of the rooms has a fireplace, leave the flue opening free or insert an air brick in the flue at ceiling level to encourage the general movement of air.

Because heat rises from basements, skirting-heating works particularly well. I have a basement dining-room and have built a long wall-to-wall slate-topped serving unit giving it a recessed base which houses a skirting radiator for its entire length. In this way, heat is spread across the floor and yet the radiator itself is barely visible. Where kitchen units are wall-hung or are being specially designed and built in, the same treatment could apply. Otherwise, with a hot water system, choose the form of radiator that can most easily be accommodated in the general design. Where a basement is to be a totally self-contained unit, night storage radiators, the new ones which give more heat in the afternoons and evenings are particularly appropriate and, if the flat is fitted with its own White Meter, the tenant can choose just how much electricity he uses and pays for. Another possibility, more flexible but more expensive to run, is the slim electric thermo-statically-controlled skirting radiator.

A basement with area steps to the road could be converted conveniently into a self-contained flat, and the internal staircase removed completely to give more space both to the basement and ground floor. A four-storeyed house could be turned into two maisonettes with the basement and ground floor forming one unit entered into from the front area, the first and second floors forming a second unit and being entered into through the front door. When two floors form a flat, or the whole house is owned by one family, it can work well to plan the kitchen in the front part of the basement, with the dining-room at the rear, opening out through french windows to a courtyard or garden. Alternatively, you could instal a service lift, plan the dining-room directly above the kitchen and use the back basement room as a play-room for the children, close to the kitchen for meals and supervision, and opening out into the garden.

Vaults under a road, originally used for coal storage, can often be put to good use once they have been made water-tight. They might contain oil for an oil-fired boiler, provide space for a bathroom or utility room or make a grotto for shade-loving plants and, in this way, give a longer vista to the rooms inside. Sometimes, where there is no garden space at the back of the house, areas can be glassed over to form a conservatory. The back wall of the house can be opened up and the light boosted with 'day-light' fluorescent tubes.

Even though your basement may not be suitable to live in, you could use it for a central heating boiler-room, where solid fuel or an oil tank could be stored. In this room you could install a sink and washing equipment to make a self-contained laundry and drying-room.

Shallow basements, or those with some front garden, can often be converted into garages. It is simply a question of providing a sufficient run for a ramp between the pavement and the house. The fall of the ground should never be more than one in five and you should ensure that walls, ceilings and access doors all meet the appropriate fire regulations.

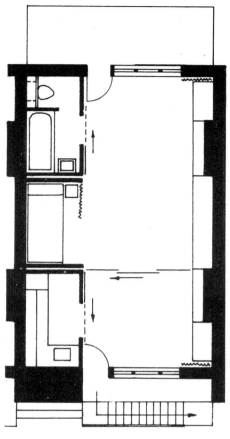

This basement plan of a terrace house gives ideas for making a self-contained flat with its own access via the area steps. The area is opened up, with its cross wall removed entirely, to make one long through living-room with sliding screens to break it up as required. Kitchen, sleeping recess and bathroom flank one side, the other wall with fireplaces blocked off is fitted with a bank of valuable storage. The back door opens into a small garden linked with steps to the main garden at a higher level

The constricted space of the medium-sized terrace house has been exploded in this conversion by architect John Winter. Most of the floor has been sacrificed to gain a remarkable double-storey room approaching twenty feet in height. With the dividing wall opened up, there is one large basement area (opposite, above) which combines sitting-room, dining-room and kitchen, with a bay window at one end and a huge fourteen-foot-high window, which rises up into the ground floor, at the other. By opening up the staircase well on both floors, a sense of spaciousness pervades the whole house. The downstairs living area is far larger than it at first appears — it goes right through the house and is over thirty feet long and twenty feet wide. A tile-topped room-divider makes a handsome serving counter between the kitchen and the dining area, which is large enough to accommodate a table and eight Magistretti chairs. Beyond that, by the huge window, are a sofa and chairs. The basement area is linked to the gallery by a wooden staircase (above). A view of part of the living area from the gallery, is shown opposite, below. The owners have retained the ground-floor front room as a more formal sitting-room, but on party nights, with its double doors open on to the gallery, the space is adequate for any demands

This Pimlico basement hadn't been lived in for over thirty years and carried an official closing order when architects Roy Stout and Patrick Litchfield took over the mid-Victorian house of which it is a part. The two architects have divided the house up to provide themselves with homes and office space. The self-contained maisonette in the basement and on part of the ground floor is used by Patrick Litchfield. As it is a corner house the basement area, some four feet wide, continued round into the side street, and under the pavement were eight vaulted cellars opening into it. The basement has been opened up to provide one large living space, incorporating the kitchen but making use of the linked vaults as additional spaces. The suspended slatted ceiling in the main area (opposite) conceals the structural beams and emphasises further the vistas created through the floor-to-ceiling windows to the opened-up vaults beyond. The use of heather brown quarry tiles throughout is a further unifying factor. The front walls of the vaults which separated them from the areas were removed; they are now painted white and most are filled with shade-loving plants. Thus exposed, they have become a sort of arcaded garden (left) and, especially when lit at night, their back walls seem to be the real enclosure of the living-room

The kitchen (opposite, below) which forms part of the main living area is partially screened by the chest-high Iroko and black formica working surface. Additional working space is provided by the flap-down front of the storage unit seen to the left of the picture. The eye-level grill/oven is neatly fitted in a structural column which also houses the television set on the other side (opposite, above).

When the side wall of the house was buttressed (see page 162) it was necessary to build down into the basement area: this enabled two of the vaults to be joined directly into the main basement space. One is used as a dining alcove (right, above), the other as a tiny spare bedroom (right, below)

The original, major conversion of the basement of this Early Victorian house, into a dining-room and kitchen, was by architect John Prizeman (see page 90). Later the area was further opened up by architect Maya Hambly into one kitchen-dining area which covers the whole floor, and lets the light from the glazed ends flow freely through the space. An unbroken wall of equipment and storage fittings runs from front to back (right) and a continuous floor of sealed-cork tiles further unifies the space. At the back, the glazed opening (shown above and below) leads into a small walled garden

Two basements opened up to provide linked dining-kitchen areas: in both cases original features have been preserved to make a contribution to the newly-converted space.

The kitchen and dining-room shown on the left was converted by architect Joyce Lowrie from a coal cellar and store in the basement of her Oxford terrace house. The dining-room is at the back of the house with french doors, leading up into a paved garden. The long serving counter is topped by a slab of black slate. A skirting radiator runs as a recessed plinth the full length of the cupboards. Louvred doors were chosen for the cupboards partly to allow the old walls to dry out thoroughly; for this reason also the rough brick and stone surfaces were left unplastered and simply painted. The existing quarry tiles were retained and the colour and texture of these matched through in the vinyl flooring of the kitchen beyond. All the other ingredients, sealed pine, white paint and slate working tops, are repeated in the kitchen so that when the sliding door is open the two spaces relate.

Architect Tom Manning converted the basement of a house in Twickenham (right, above and below) by the simple device of making a large opening in the dividing wall between the front and back rooms. This brings in added light and a greater feeling of space as well as simplifying the serving and clearing up of meals. On formal occasions folding doors can separate the rooms. The structural and architectural character of the basement has been left much as it stood. The quarry tiles of the kitchen floor are turned up to form the face of the plinths of the kitchen units. Strip-lighting, set beneath the wall-hung cupboards, floods light down on to the working surfaces

The basement of this Early Victorian terrace house was converted by architect John Smith into an open living area incorporating a kitchen and space for children to play, and with access to the garden. The picture above shows the sitting and dining sections of the area with a glimpse of the kitchen beyond the stairs. The middle dividing wall was entirely removed and replaced by a beam which spans from wall to wall. The old staircase ran from the front to the back of the house. This was

removed to make space for a utility
and boiler-room and the new open
stair built to lie across the house in
the new basement room. All walls
and paintwork are white to unify
the space, and cork tiles are used as
a floor finish for the entire area

Roof space, of course, can offer all sorts of possibilities for enlarging your living space. Even simply boarded over, with a retractable roof ladder, it can provide valuable and easily-accessible storage. Retractable roof ladders, made in timber and aluminium, are easy to manipulate and ensure that you use your roof space to the full. Otherwise, the effort of carrying a ladder all the way upstairs just results in things lying and collecting dust year after year. If you want to use the roof space for storing, it is well worth boarding over the floor in some way. Not only does this help to spread the load, but it makes it easier to move about at the same time and increases the insulation against heat loss from the rooms below. If you want to do this, pack the joists to the top with loose-fill or mineral quilt and cover with sheets of chipboard or ordinary floor-boards. As ceiling joists aren't intended to take the load of heavy trunks and people walking on them you should be very careful not to overload your roof in the main central part. It is best to store in the angle made by the roof, as this is the point at which the joists can carry their greatest load. Where the tiles or slates have no lining or insulation beneath them, and you are not proposing to re-roof the house, you should fix some lining material to the underside of the rafters. This can simply be polythene sheet tacked on with stout drawing pins which will keep out the damp, or rigid panels of flame-resistant polystyrene which will keep out cold as well as damp.

If you don't want to use the roof space for anything, it is enough just to pack insulation material – quilt or loose-fill – between the joists, but remember that, by doing this, you will be stopping any heat from rising to keep the cold water storage tank unfrozen, so be sure that it is boxed in or given an insulating jacket of some kind.

Even without sufficient space to make them fully habitable, roofs can be put to good use as playrooms for young children or dens for

Composer Richard Rodney Bennett in converting the attic floor of his house in Islington into a work-room studio overcame the problems posed by pokey windows and sloping ceilings. An interesting flow of light and space has been created by painting walls and ceilings white, and covering the floor with white vinyl tiles. As a result the tiny amount of incoming light is bounced and reflected off every possible sur-face. A similar lighting effect is obtained at night by the use of well-positioned spots. To the left, floor-to-ceiling cupboards have been incorporated unobtrusively into the general scheme

older ones. To use your roof space in this way, it may be enough to put in an extendable ladder-stair, and line it thoroughly with 2-inch thick fire-resistant polystyrene insulating panels. The ceiling joists of the rooms below will usually need doubling up to make them sufficiently safe to take a floor. This simpler form of adaptation doesn't demand dormer windows. The insertion of rooflights should be sufficient. The best I know of are Velux, the double-glazed type that don't leak. If you run benches below these, you will find that the lack of ceiling height won't matter. Blocking off the base of the roof slope with cupboards will provide storage and reduce the volume of space to be heated.

Where space allows, better access than a loft ladder is definitely worth having. Circular staircases can help here, but they can be expensive unless you are lucky enough to pick up a cheap second-hand one. A steep, fixed ladder-stair is generally permitted for roof space not classified as 'habitable'. For a 'habitable' room, however, the angle of a straight flight must not be steeper than 42 degrees, and the entrance into the converted space must give you headroom of 6 feet 6 inches, as you step off the last tread. The slope of the roof can sometimes be exploited when fitting in stairs and the stair set to run up under it. This can be useful both with single flights and dog legs (that is, when the direction of the stair turns 180 degrees by means of a half-landing).

If you need an entire floor of extra space and have a house with a parapet which screens the roof behind it from the road, it may be possible to rebuild the roof structure to give rooms with normal ceiling height throughout. If the face of the new front and back walls are set back a little, they can be given french or sliding glazed doors so that the space in front forms a small balcony. The parapet will provide a useful balustrade. This has been done most attractively in a number of houses in Eaton Square, London. We show another example on page 122.

Houses without parapets often provide additional living-space without the roof form being altered. One London-based firm, Attica, contend that so long as the house has a ridge height of 9 feet, conversion is usually possible. For a 'habitable' room – a full-time bedroom or living-room, for example – local authorities demand that the major part of the roof space is a minimum 7 feet 6 inches high. By extending the flat part of the ceiling, dormer windows often make this height a possibility. Remember that these can be glazed at the sides as well as at the front to give better penetration of light.

There is another kind of dormer window – an inverted dormer – where the face of the window (which can be glazed to floor level) is set inside the slope of the roof, and the roof structure in front cut away to form a balcony. This treatment can add character to an attic (see page 114). Inverted dormers can open up the roof space to views and sun, give you an opportunity to do some planting and fit full-length windows which would otherwise tend to induce vertigo at this level.

Using the top of the house for roof gardens and balconies is becoming a much more practical possibility since clean air regulations have come into force. Where the roof structure is in a bad state, it may be worth building a completely new structure to house a whole flat or an additional floor. A parapet forming a balustrade to a shallow balcony on the front road side could maintain the appearance of a façade. In one case, someone without a garden had a pitched roof in such a crumbling condition that it needed complete re-building and she decided to do this by making half a large roof garden, the other half a large room, flat-roofed with glass sliding doors. In this room she fitted a small stainless sink and power points into one corner. This made it a perfect place for her two small children to play on sunny days, or for herself and her husband to entertain on summer evenings.

If you want to use some of your house to bring you in an income, it is best to use the lower floors as flats and to live at the top of the house yourself. Otherwise, unless you have separate access, it does mean that the main stairs will be used by the flat occupant and will demand special fire-proofing. You can often maintain access to the garden by external spiral stairs from balconies. These provide valuable additional fire-escapes. Re-made attic floors are perhaps most useful as a means of finding privacy, and can be turned into studios, studies and work-rooms of every kind. They are also very useful as living or play space for children once they have got beyond the stage of needing supervision all the time. They can be useful to store equipment (especially if you haven't a basement) which would otherwise take up useful space on the lower floors of the house. A friend of mine has even had a large gas-fired boiler installed on the top floor. This has a balanced flue so it simply sits against an outside wall. She has also created a laundry area out of the top landing, with a bank of equipment – washing-machine, tumble-dryer, ironing equipment, and so on – all hidden behind folding, sliding louvred doors.

There is one other way in which roof space can be exploited to gain more living space, even though the roof itself is not very high. This is by opening up the ceiling of one of the rooms below into the roof space and lining the underside of the rafters so that they provide a new ceiling, and then building a sleeping gallery, a half or a third of the way across the floor space and reached by a ladder-stair. This would enlarge a small bedroom for a teenager into a really useful bedsitter with lots of room for housing books, hobbies and so on. A roof-light could light the gallery and would add to the quality of light in the room as a whole. The ceiling joists themselves can support the gallery; whether or not they will need stiffening will depend on their size and the direction in which they run.

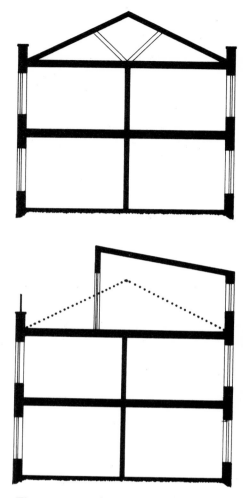

The top section shows a typical roof structure, insufficiently tall to convert into extra living space as it stands. The section below illustrates a possible conversion method where more space is wanted, or where the roof is in such poor condition as to warrant remaking. The existing back wall of the house is extended upwards to form the back wall of the new floor. The front wall has sliding glass doors opening on to a roof terrace. The existing parapet forms the base for the terrace balustrade

If you do develop the attic you have got to bring up services to make it warm and light. Electricity, of course, is no problem and if it doesn't suit you to extend the main heating of the house up there, thermostatically-controlled skirting heaters or oil-filled radiators are a good choice as they are light and can be screwed safely to the walls. Heat always rises, so once it is opened up, this is a part of the house that is not likely to get cold. But unless the attic space, once opened up, is thoroughly insulated, cold air does form and this can make the lower floors of the house feel cold. Getting mains water to the top of the house is no trouble, but if you want to tuck a bathroom in the attic, you will have to push the cold-water tank as high as possible in the ridge space to get a sufficient head of water for a bath. Even then, it will probably not give you the minimum 3 feet over the shower head necessary for a shower. The solution to this is to use an independent instantaneous or storage heater, worked directly off the mains, and linked with a shower head. These heaters incorporate a special kind of valve which reduces water pressure.

To place a den or simple storage space in your loft will probably require no more than to call in a reliable local builder. If you are a handyman, it is the sort of job you could do yourself. But for anything more complicated – certainly if you want 'habitable' rooms – you should commission an architect to advise you because the building regulations are very complicated. More simply, you can go to one of the firms which specialize in loft conversions. Most of these firms make no charge for coming to survey the possibilities of your loft. From then on, the whole thing is in their hands. Their design departments get out a scheme and look after planning and building applications. Because they provide their own skilled tradesmen, the job is usually carried out far more quickly than could be done by the average small builder. Some firms claim they can complete in as little as two or three weeks, once all the details have been settled.

These specialist firms undoubtedly do a very useful job, but it is still up to you to be clear-cut about design standards. If dormer windows are to be installed, insist that the frames and glazing match exactly the windows of the rest of the house. Only in that way will the house retain its unity. Where dormers are traditional, see that the external treatment matches others, as far as possible, to be found locally in houses of the same period. Modern dormers are too often festooned with unnecessary gutters and rainwater pipes. A structural tip worth bearing in mind is that, if the dormer roof is tilted backwards a little, a gutter is quite unnecessary.

Where windows are set behind parapets and are virtually screened from the road then, of course, you can choose whatever is most appropriate to the rooms inside.

Architect Michael Willis has made a maisonette for himself at the top of a Wimpole Street house. Apart from a small bathroom the whole of the top floor has been given up to make one large sitting-room. Partition walls were knocked down and replaced by sliding glass doors which open the space up visually to take in the staircase well. The staircase has a top light which floods additional light in to the sitting-room. The original timber sash windows were defective and have been replaced by aluminium ones which keep to the same slim sections. The room is contained by the slope of the Mansard roof and the windows are fitted with roller blinds instead of curtains. Vinyl sheeting covers the entire floor and runs up over the structural plinth at the base of the windowed wall. Honey-coloured hessian covers the walls and ceiling giving the room a soft warm light. The kitchen, dining-room and bedroom are on the floor below

The roof space of a house in Earl's Court was converted into this flat by the owner, architect Michael Manser. A small terrace was created by cutting back into the slope of the roof and inserting an inverted dormer. By giving the dormer glazed sides, more light is able to penetrate into the room and at the same time long, interesting vistas have been opened up across the whole floor. The structure is left undisguised and pale finishes are used everywhere to reflect as much light as possible. The use of white carpeting and the light furniture further enhances the effect. A low bank of shelves and cupboards is tucked into the angle of roof and floor making use of all available space

It is not necessary to build dormer windows to get light into attic space. Here two architects show how they solved the problem by simply slotting glass into the roof structure along the length of the room.

The conservatory, shown above, provides a quiet retreat under the roof of a Boston waterfront building, converted by architect Gerard Cugini. The wall-to-wall skylight opens up a view of the whole city and on sunny days it floods the room with sunlight. Three walls have been fitted with built-in banquettes and shelves for books and music equipment.

The attic flat, shown opposite, was converted out of the unwanted roof space over a block of shops and offices in the centre of Copenhagen by Danish architect-owner, Finn Groes-Petersen. It provided an area of over 1,600 feet — roughly that of a medium-sized house. The plan is basically an immense living area with a kitchen at one end. The

bedroom and small adjoining bathroom have been inserted at gallery level and are approached by a wooden staircase. The architect wanted to avoid the intrusion of a great modern dormer window into the high tiled roof of the house; instead he slotted strip windows between the great roof timbers. The sombre brick walls have been painted white; the sturdy posts and beams, at least a couple of centuries old, have been repaired and polished

The roof space of an old house in Bordeaux was converted into this splendid flat, but the ideas could be applied to any roof space of similar scale. Architect Michel Sadirac has retained as many of the structural features as possible, both to provide dramatic visual interest and to keep building costs to a minimum. To avoid a visual surfeit of beams, and overcome a problem common with attics of excessive heat and cold, a false ceiling was installed, insulated by mineral wool. Existing roof timbers dramatically cut across the interior of the living and dining areas, shown here. Most of the furniture has been built in or set along the walls as it was felt that the beams were a sufficiently divisive feature without introducing further visual complications with isolated groups of furniture. Areas of brilliant colour contrast with the lacquered paintwork of beams and joists, and the matt white rough-textured walls

This once pokey attic in a Victorian terrace house was transformed into a snug and inviting bedroom by lining the walls and ceiling in traditional manner with tongued-and-grooved pine boarding. The boarding acts as splendid insulation as well as contributing colour and texture to the tiny space. The line of the boards emphasizes the direction of the contrasting planes. The rich but simple character has been echoed in the pine and painted furniture, the shaggy goatskin rug and the crocheted cover. A mirror is set opposite the dormer window to reflect more light, and the base of the bed is built in

This hideaway bed-sitting room forms part of an attic floor added to a Kensington house by architect Edward Samuel. In this case the pine boarding used to line the ceiling is set horizontally to spread the space visually and offset the sharp angle of the pitch. By glazing the cheeks of the new dormer window it was possible to keep it small enough not to overwhelm the traditional Georgian façade below. This is a useful trick which can be applied to existing dormers to increase the penetration of light into attic rooms. A locker bench fills in the awkward corner at the lower end of the slope

In a house where the roof is set behind a parapet wall it is often possible to convert the original roof structure into an additional room as architect Bill Siddons has done in the house shown here. Floor-to-ceiling windows stretch from wall to wall at one end of the newly constructed room, and a long rectangular skylight floods light down through the stair well. Here, and in other conversions of this kind, the freedom from partition walls, and the sweeping views make this space the obvious choice for daytime living. Bedrooms and bathrooms are on the floor below. The front of the new living area has been set back some three or four feet from the main façade; the original parapet acts as a balustrade and prevents any feelings of vertigo caused by such low windows

When their children left home, architectural journalist Malcolm MacEwen and his wife Ann, an architect and town planner, converted the roof space and top floor of their late-Victorian house, into a maisonette for themselves, and the lower three floors into self-contained flats. Architect, John Winter, was asked to carry out the job, and the new terrace and living-dining-kitchen area that he constructed from the roof space of the house are shown here. Bedrooms and bathrooms are on the floor below. Full advantage was taken of the fine views over Parliament Hill Fields by the use of big double-glazed windows and by introducing a terrace to catch the south-west sun. In the living area (opposite, above) a bank of shelves and cupboards was built along the wall which backs on to the roof space of the adjoining house: in addition to providing valuable storage space the shelves serve as effective insulation against heat loss. The kitchen and dining area (opposite, below) are separated by the double-sink unit which also provides a pass-through hatch for serving meals. A ceiling of tongued-and-grooved pine unifies the whole; the floor in the living-dining area is maple strip; vinyl tiles have been used in the kitchen

THE KITCHEN

The best place for a kitchen, its size and character, clearly depends on the way you live. If you have a traditionally terraced house, and you don't want to do anything else with the basement, a solution that works well – and which appears in some of the examples in this book – is to use the front of the basement as a kitchen. You will then be close by for mains services, access for tradesmen, dustbins and, at the same time, can enjoy some of the life of the street. This may mean cutting back an area but, with walls painted white and hung with climbing flowering plants, it needn't be gloomy to look out on.

The back room, especially if you open it up with french doors to the garden, can then provide a conveniently adjacent dining-room. If this is given a fairly informal character, it can be an extremely useful family room – a place for television, for sewing and where young children can play.

This demands a large sturdy table with a good light over it, so that it can be used for painting or jigsaws on wet days, or as a place where the older ones can do their prep. Where such dining-rooms sometimes need to look formal, it is worth having a bank of storage cupboards – wall-to-wall, floor-to-ceiling – into which all the clutter, such as the sewing machine, television and children's books and toys, can vanish in a moment.

The two rooms can be linked by a wide sliding door, but a hatch could do a similar job. With this sort of link it is possible for someone to be working in the kitchen, while keeping an eye on young children at the same time. In fine weather, the children can be in the garden and still near at hand. You may find it more useful to make the back room the kitchen if it is especially large and can be used for informal family meals as well. Then the front of the basement could act as a formal dining-room which could perhaps double as a study.

Where there is a back extension, the kitchen is often housed here,

The handsome ground-floor living-room in an 1830's house in Canonbury was converted into this splendid kitchen-dining area designed and made by Michael Wickham. The storage and shelving units are in solid ash; the brown-tiled working area is U-shaped with a logical sequence of prepare, cook and serve, and the serving unit, with its open shelves, effectively defines the two areas. The units are set on a recessed raised plinth which is continued through the bank of cupboards on the right hand side. Refrigerator and oven are incorporated in this storage bank just out of the main working area. The dining table of pine was also made by Michael Wickham. The floor throughout is cork tiles

126

and certainly if it is big enough for a counter or a small table for informal meals this can work usefully where there is no basement. The two ground-floor rooms can then be opened up into one, with the back part used for more formal dinner parties. This does allow the house-wife, or whoever is working in the kitchen, to enjoy the garden. One advantage of having the kitchen at garden level, or at least accessible by means of shallow steps, is that it does make it easier to have drinks and meals outside in warm weather.

Where the basement is to provide a self-contained flat, another solution is to have the kitchen at the back on the ground floor, linked, if possible, with the garden by a balcony and steps. It is usually the smaller of the two rooms, and the larger one in front can then be used as a dining-room or dining/playroom or dining-room/study. In small houses of two or three floors, the back room might be subdivided for cooking and eating so that the front room can be used as a sitting-room.

Another way of fitting in a kitchen has been most successfully carried out by an architect in Highgate. He had a large semi-detached Victorian house with a porch and front door on the front façade. He removed the porch and converted the front door into a window match-ing those on the same side of the house, making a new porch, opening into the house mid-way along the side wall. As a result, the front door now enters directly into the staircase lobby and the large front entrance-hall has been turned into a compact modern kitchen. The kitchen was formerly in the basement and, in this new position, is linked directly and more conveniently with the big double living-room on the ground floor.

Although the basement headroom might be sufficient to allow a kitchen to be installed, it is sometimes unacceptable under Building Regulations for use as a dining-room. Having the kitchen and dining-room on separate floors can be tiresome, but so long as you can manage family meals in the kitchen, a small service life built into one of the side recesses of the chimney in the dining-room can handle more formal meals, especially if you have an *au pair* or help in for dinner parties. In fact a lift in this position can also link a basement dining-room with a ground-floor sitting-room, as this will greatly simplify drinks and tea parties.

Apart from those kitchens large enough to eat in, and kitchens linked with separate dining-rooms, you may have the space for a tiny supplementary kitchen that is little more than a bank of cupboards – the sort that would fit into a *pied à terre* or where there is a large room at the top of a house used for entertaining. In such a room, a small stainless-steel sink, a fridge for ice and drinks, an electric kettle, coffee-pot and toaster, plus one or two hot-plates sunk into a slate top, can make entertaining more fun for the hostess. A kitchen of this kind is also worth considering if teenagers, an *au pair* or nanny are all living at the top of the house, or if you have a lot of week-end guests. A recess on an upper landing can be successfully fitted up in this way, too. It can even be linked with a washing-machine and airing cupboard, and used to house all the cleaning equipment for the upper floors so that you avoid having to trail down to the basement kitchen every time you want to make a cup of tea.

If you are employing an architect to convert your house, you will probably get him to design the kitchen in detail for you as well. However, if you are not using an architect, it is worth considering one of the free services offered by the manufacturers of kitchen units. But, however good their design department is, you are likely to be disappointed with the result unless you sort out your needs pretty thoroughly before approaching them.

You must be clear in your mind about the way you want to use your kitchen. If you are a cooking enthusiast, for instance, you obviously need more room and a very different kind of room from somebody who likes spending as little time in the kitchen as possible. It's very important to think seriously about automatic equipment at this stage, and to challenge any prejudices against it. It is no good deciding that a washing-up machine is a must in your life six months after your built-in kitchen has been completed. Automatic equipment can save an enormous amount of space and simplify planning in so many ways. If fully automatic washing-up and washing-machines are independently plumbed in, they make no demands on the water supply to the sink and can be set some distance from it. If you have to wash clothes in the kitchen, a practice one should try to avoid, at least a fully automatic washing-machine, ideally incorporating a tumble-dryer as well, enables the whole operation to be completely self-contained. An independently plumbed-in washing-up machine need not be near the main sink at all but could be set under the serving hatch or by the door leading to the dining-room with its own small sink and waste-disposal unit.

If you think you might ever want a waste-disposal unit, you certainly should fit a double sink and one of the sinks should have the kind of waste that can be adapted for one. Waste disposal units seem to have a particular relevance in towns – in country or suburban gardens one can lose so much waste to a compost heap – but in town, particularly in hot weather or with central heating, it can become an unsavoury problem. Hygiene apart, it certainly makes vegetable preparation simpler if you prepare them in the sink with a waste unit and simply flush away the peelings when the job is done.

A double sink with double drainers is essential in any kitchen unless you have a plumbed-in dishwasher. Double sinks and drainers need not take up so much space. Sissons make one model which is only 3 feet 6 inches wide and could be fitted into the smallest kitchen. Or the second sink can be narrower but as deep as the main sink to reduce the overall width. Never let a kitchen planner bully you into accepting sinks without draining – or at least stacking – space on both sides, unless the sink top is sunk into the surrounding working surface. Otherwise, you will have a tiresome crack between the edge of the sink and the adjacent working surface down which water will trickle and crumbs fall.

Dishwashers are gaining greater acceptance. For anyone with a family or who entertains a great deal, they not only save time and enable you to avoid a dreary job but can help keep the kitchen cleaner and tidier. They certainly do a better job of washing up than most people do, although to work at their most effective they need softened water. This saves a lot of detergent and everything comes out of the machine much shinier. In addition, the motor of such equipment should last longer because the immersion heater is not fighting the deposit of lime that builds up with hard water. (Hard water is dealt with as a subject under *Services*.)

Whatever the size and shape of your kitchen, you must insist that there is a proper work flow for cooking. The basic sequence is Store-Prepare-Cook-Serve, with no physical break between the boiling rings and the sink. You should aim at a continuous run of working surface, sink, working surface, cooker (hob unit), working surface. There should be no interruption of doors, or units, such as refrigerators or waist-level ovens, rising up above the working-top level. According to the Royal Society for the Prevention of Accidents, such breaks of flow are the cause of most of the worst accidents in the home. The best independent kitchen designers all endorse these rules, and, interestingly, the National House Builders' Registration Council has made this the basic layout for its members to follow.

For this reason, your cooker hob should have a surface on both sides on to which pots can be safely drawn. Laminated plastic is an invaluable material for work-tops, but it is not the best material to place adjacent to cooker-tops as it cannot reliably take really hot saucepans, and for safety in the kitchen this is essential. It is dangerous to have to grope around for asbestos mats or to stagger to your stainless-steel draining board. This is the way accidents occur. On either side of your cooker, you should have some material such as stone, marble, slate, Eternit (black asbestos cement which looks like slate), or stainless steel that can take extreme heat.

Another useful point to remember is that many pieces of essential kitchen equipment don't need to be closely linked to sink and hob. If you separate the oven from the boiling rings, it will leave cupboard space below the hob for saucepans and other cooking utensils, and the oven can be more comfortably accessible at waist level outside the main working sequence. Oven-cooked food needs little attention, but again you must have a work-top next to it which can take a hot casserole and onto which you can transfer the joint from its roasting tray to the carving-dish before taking it into the dining-room. This argues for a separate oven being linked with the main serving-area. If you have a deep-freezer separate from your refrigerator, you may well be able to manage with a waist-high model refrigerator or to use a wall-hung version such as the one by Bosch with double doors. It could be fitted directly over the sink, or your main preparation area. Even an electric mixer can reduce the amount of working surface you need, as the number of mixing bowls needed is so much less.

Before you hand your kitchen over to the planners, another point to consider is whether it would improve the working layout if you could block up a door completely or perhaps use the top half of it as a hatchway or another window if it opens to the outside. Is there a larder or a cupboard in your kitchen that could go? A larder, as such, is not necessary, as air bricks in a wall-hung cupboard or a cupboard beneath the working surface will give you all the space you need for food such as fresh vegetables, yesterday's joint, the remains of a trifle, etc. Too many people keep completely inappropriate food in larders. Tinned and packaged goods, jam and so on can all be kept in dry, unventilated cupboards.

Compactness is the thing to aim for in your essential cooking area, whether you have a tiny kitchen or one 20 feet square. If your kitchen is a large one, it is far better to group all the equipment into a small operational area and to develop the rest of the room into a pleasant place for family meals, children's play, dressmaking, etc. If the room is large enough, there could be room for a laundry corner with its own separate sink as well.

Ideally, washing and cooking activities should be separated. If you can, find a recess in a bathroom, downstairs cloakroom or utility room for your washing machine. It is an advantage to link it with a sink as, with most machines, a small amount of washing can be done by hand in the sink and the clothes simply spun dry in the machine. But if your house is very small, or you are equipping a flat, with no alternative to putting the washing machine in the kitchen, do plumb it in completely and have, if possible, one that incorporates a tumbler drier, such as the Bendix, so that the total operation of washing and drying is done before you remove the clothes from the machine. A front-opening machine can usually be slid under a work-top, which makes it less demanding in the lay-out. This argument apart, top-opening ones do leave you free to use any detergent you like and accidentally opening them isn't so disastrous. You can also stop the cycle at any time. However, if you are installing either type in anything but the basement (or ground floor, if there is no basement below), there is a lot to be said for standing them in a zinc tray with its own waste.

Where to go for advice and help

The Design Centre and the London and Regional Building Centres, and many of the large stores have kitchen exhibitions from time to time, incorporating a great variety of merchandise. Permanently open are:

The Kitchen and Bathroom Centre,
    22 Conduit Street, London W1
Thorn Kitchen Advisory Centre,
    Upper St Martin's Lane, London WC2
The Westinghouse Kitchen Centre,
    Berners Street, London W1

The English Rose Kitchen Planning Centre,
   Charles Street, Warwick
Multyflex Kitchens Ltd, Design and Planning Centre,
   Modular Works, Dafen, Llanelli, Carms.
The following firms provide advisory or planning services:
   Grovewood Products Ltd, Tipton, Staffordshire
   Hygena Ltd, Kirby Trading Estate, Liverpool
   Kandya Ltd, Pump Lane, Hayes, Middlesex
   W. H. Paul Ltd, Breeston, Derbyshire
   Christian Sell, 45 Camden Passage, London W1
Wrighton Distributors provide a planning service in all leading towns.

By clever planning, architect Bill Siddons converted this small back room of a typical terrace house to provide space for both cooking and eating. The working area is long and U-shaped; at the narrow end is a gas hob with ducted hood over, which exploits the otherwise unused flue of the room's fireplace. The built-in oven is set over the refrigerator (above) and a double stainless-steel sink forms part of the counter which separates the kitchen and dining areas. In this position it faces towards the french doors which lead into the garden, and enables used dishes to be cleared directly on to it for washing up

Timber can be used with great effect in kitchens where space is limited, to help give unity to the overall design, at the same time providing a sympathetic decorative feature. The two treatments on these pages show what different effects can be achieved by the skilful use of wood panelling.

The kitchen on the left comes from the New York house of textile-designer Jack Larsen. The old barn timbers used to line the walls give the room a pleasant rustic flavour, and at the same time provide an ideal surface for hanging copper pans, basket-wear, etc.

Timber has also been used effectively in the small kitchen-dining-room (above) designed by architect Philip Pank. The all-purpose shelving units are of solid ash-veneered plywood with coved solid teak tops. The upper range of shelves incorporates the cooker hood and the walls are lined with horizontal boarding

The designers of the two kitchens shown here were both faced at the outset with an awkward room-shape, but the imaginative use of simple treatments has resulted, in each case, in a compact, well-planned kitchen.

The awkward shape of the London kitchen, shown opposite, has been imaginatively dealt with by designer Philip Jebb. The tight little recess in front of the window has been used as a U-shaped preparation corner. The electric hob is set at the corner of the work top allowing the boiling rings to be accessible from two sides. Blue and white Wrighton's units provide strong colour which helps to unify the scheme. The printed blind is a pretty alternative to curtains.

Designer Liz Goldfinger was asked to transform the long narrow room with a window at one end (above and below), into a workable kitchen. To save the expense of altering the existing plumbing, a long narrow counter was built the whole length of the chimney-breast wall. In order to utilize the two recesses a drain tray for the double sink was set within one recess, leaving the adjacent work-top free for preparation of food. The other recess provided space for a raised shelf for 'dumping', again leaving the work-top free. Drawer and cupboard units built-in under the worktops provide space for storing cooking utensils and a rubbish container. To avoid cluttering the circulation area the kitchen door was removed from its hinges and hung from sliding door gear. Worktop surround to sink bowls is in Afzelia; hard-wood worktop adjacent to the cooker is in Eternith, which is heat-proof

Well-designed storage units incorporating the main items of kitchen equipment (refrigerator, waist-high oven/grill), such as those shown here, make the best use of all available space, and also ensure maximum efficiency.

A kitchen designed by architect Edward Samuel in a house he converted in Hampstead is shown opposite, above. The whole treatment has a pleasant sturdiness which relates well to the old room. The gas hob is set into a worktop of tiles which are continued up the wall behind it. The hood over it is incorporated into a range of open

shelves from which concealed light floods down onto the working surface. The cupboards were designed by Edward Samuel; framing is of pine, the panels are cork veneer.

Wood veneer has been used by architect John Smith, in the kitchen shown opposite, below, to provide sleek, easily cleaned surfaces which contribute warmth and colour to the room. The double oven and refrigerator are built in a bank of storage, and a rack for wine bottles is housed over the refrigerator. The working surface to the left of the oven is backed by blackboard panel for messages and reminders. The

deep facia of the shelf above conceals a fluorescent tube. This treatment is echoed in the serving unit to the right. Sink and cooking hob are at the other end of the room.

The small corridor-shaped kitchen above, open to the dining-room which lies beyond, was designed by Godfrey and George Grima. The elegant units are custom-built and have formica working surfaces. Instead of a separate hob unit individual Creda boiling rings have been set in the worktop with a ducted hood over. The oven is in the unit separating dining-room and kitchen

An extension of the kitchen makes a conveniently accessible playroom which doubles as a dining area, in the Wimbledon house shown opposite, above. The garden, reached through french windows leading directly from the playroom, becomes a further extension in good weather. The waist-high counter top and gate enables small children to be close to whoever is looking after them without being under their feet.

The kitchen-dining-room by architect Edward Samuel (opposite, below) was designed essentially for family living, yet it retains a pleasant orderliness made necessary by the fact that it opens on to the living-room.

The window wall of the small kitchen in Kingston (right, above) designed by Unit Five was purposely kept clear of fitments so that the view over the garden could be enjoyed from as many angles as possible. The opening section is fitted with Crittall louvres to give maximum ventilation and rough-textured brown glass is set into the arch over. The ceiling is dropped over the dining area and the cylindrical fitting, set in the lowered ceiling, floods light down on to the table

The kitchen in a late-Victorian house in Hampstead, shown right, below, was designed by architect Raymond Smith with room for eating as well. The work bench with its boarded cupboards doubles conveniently as a serving table. Most of the cooking equipment is hidden behind sliding panels

Architect Timothy Rendle designed the kitchen/dining-room shown opposite as part of the overall modernization in a house in Belgravia. In it he made the dining-table and kitchen worktops at the same level by raising the banquette seating onto a six-inch platform. With the removal of the stacking chairs, the table top can become an extension of the main working surface. In this small area the continuous working surface is not only more convenient but more restful to the eye than a change of level would be. Two double gas hob units, sink, refrigerator, dish-washing-machine, cutlery drawers, and slide-out chopping-board, are all incorporated in and under the $1\frac{1}{4}$-inch oiled beech top. Concealed strip lights illuminate the worktop. The eye-level oven unit is built into a wall, away from the working-area.

Designer Liz Goldfinger's problem was to modernize a dark, poky kitchen in the basement flat of a large, late-Victorian house, and to provide an adjacent family eating area. Her solution is shown right, above and below. The wall cutting off the kitchen from the main corridor was removed and units were built all round the room. A good working sequence has been achieved and although space is short, room has been found for a double sink, and a heat-proof surface to the right of the hob. The split-level oven and refrigerator form a bank on the right-hand side of the sink out of the main working area. The ceiling was lowered to 8 feet with a white-painted tongued-and-grooved boarded ceiling; this also runs through to the dining-recess uniting the two areas. The ducting for the extractor fan was fitted into the space above, an important feature in an open kitchen of this type. Lighting is by recessed fittings in the lowered ceiling, and concealed strip lighting

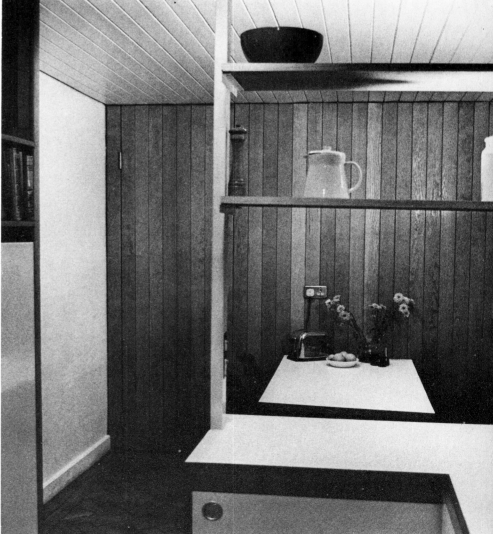

Simplicity of design coupled with the use of smooth-textured materials for horizontal and vertical surfaces have helped to make the two generous-sized kitchens shown here into elegant, harmonious rooms.

Shown above is the cooking end of a multi-purpose living area, designed by architect Patrick Fouquet for his own flat — the attic floor of a nineteenth-century house in Bordeaux. The room is kept completely simple with smooth, unbroken surfaces throughout. Oven and fridge are seen built into the right hand side wall. The white venetian blind conceals a wall-long working counter, which incorporates an independent hob unit and a double sink. Open shelves above are conveniently accessible and because of the venetian blinds their contents are concealed when they are not in use. Additional storage is provided by the waist-high bank of cupboards and drawers below the working counter. The kitchen area is divided from the sitting area by the white dining table placed at right angles to the wall.

Illustrator Allan Manham designed the kitchen/dining area, opposite, of his large-roomed Edwardian house in Barnes by linking two rooms. The wall between the rooms was opened up and replaced by a tiled-topped peninsular unit, which acts as a serving counter and houses the gas boiler rings. The tiles are unglazed, vitrified industrial tiles in off-white. The new kitchen units are deal-framed with white painted doors. Horizontal deal boarding was used to face the serving counter. The whole treatment is cool and uncluttered

THE BATHROOM

The house you take over may well have no bathroom proper at all — simply an ancient outside loo and a chipped clay sink in the kitchen — but local authority grants are generally available to help towards the cost of installing one (see page 31). Unless the existing plumbing really suits your purpose, don't let it hamstring your scheme. Clearly, sanitary fittings have to be related to drains and the more often you group them both on plan or on top of each other, the simpler and less expensive your piping and drainage will be. A wc needs a wide waste-pipe which is obviously more difficult to lose in the structure, but it is usually possible to fit basins, showers, etc, where you want them most.

The more basins, baths, wcs and showers you can get into the house, the more the pressure is taken off in the morning rush to work and school. This is, of course, solved most easily by finding room for two bathrooms and by using small equipment it is possible to pack a bathroom into a very small space indeed. Bathrooms don't have to be the full 7 feet 6 inches high demanded of other rooms. Clearly, for comfort one would want to make it as high as possible, but you could get by with 6 feet 9 inches, which would take a standard door and its frame and should accommodate all but giants.

Another point to consider when you are deciding where to fit bathrooms in is whether, at some future stage, you may want to break

In the bathroom conversion, opposite, architect John Prizeman used a simple but effective device to overcome the problem of over-high ceilings without destroying the original architectural features of the room. False walls were built which conceal storage cup- boards and incorporate bathroom fittings thus successfully bringing down the scale of the high-ceilinged room; the dominance of the hand-some original window is left un-changed. The splendid hand-marbled wall paper adds a brilliant touch of colour to the room

up the house into two or more units incorporating a bathroom in each. This may well be a possibility if you have a basement with outside access, and here there may be a chance to exploit the vaults that lie under the pavement.

An additional bathroom can often be packed into the top floor of the house over the staircase well by taking the stairs up another flight, building into the roof space and giving the bathroom a dormer window to achieve sufficient head height. If you already have an extension at the back of the house, you might be able to give it another floor and make a new bathroom there. If your house is deep through, you can use the central, poorest-lit, part to make a bathroom, giving it artificial ventilation with a duct and extractor fan. The ceiling can be lowered to house pipes and possibly the cold-water tank above. This could be reached by high-level doors in the adjacent bedroom or a trap in the ceiling of the bathroom itself.

Even if you haven't room for a bath as such, you may well be able to push a shower into a downstairs cloakroom. A shower should not be smaller than 2 feet 6 inches square on plan and, where there is space, a 3 foot square one is obviously more comfortable to use. Shower-trays are available in plastic, vitreous enamelled steel and the more traditional ceramic materials, and it is as well to choose one with a well ribbed base to avoid slipping.

Whatever you do, try to find room for a second wc. For hygiene's sake, you should have a basin with it, and even the narrowest cubicle can take one of Twyfords' little basins which slot into the wall thickness and project out only $2\frac{1}{2}$ inches.

Basins, and even showers, can be fitted into bedrooms to provide you with many of the amenities of a second bathroom. A long bank of floor-to-ceiling cupboards in your bedroom could house both a basin and a shower.

Any room that is to be used as a nursery for babies and small children will benefit from a basin. It can always have pressure taps to avoid the danger of children leaving taps on so that they overflow. It makes looking after a tiny baby a lot easier, and certainly a lot safer, if you have a basin in the same room as you change it and feed it. For this reason, it is worth taking mains water to the cold tap, so that feeds can be mixed and drinks made at night without trailing down to the kitchen. And when the room eventually becomes a play-room for older children, there will be water on hand for painting, pasting, and other hobbies. Such a sink might well be a shallow ceramic sink of the old-fashioned kind, big enough to bath a baby in, and take a second bowl inside it, which saves the floor from a lot of splashing.

A basin in a guest's bedroom makes for smoother visits. I have built into our guest-room a bank of waist-high cupboards, with drawers, giving it a white melamine top and sinking a simple white ceramic basin at one end. I have left space between two units for sitting up at the bench so that guests can use it as a dressing-table or to write letters, and I can use it for the sewing-machine, when having water at hand for pressing is a great advantage. Incorporated in a unit of this kind, with all the plumbing concealed in the cupboard below, the basin is barely noticeable and should overcome most people's prejudice against having basins in bedrooms. In a smaller room where you don't want to go to the trouble of building a basin into a counter, there are now several good-looking cantilevered models available, with small side shelves cast in one with the basin itself. Adamsez, Goslett and Armitage all make them.

Another way to conceal a basin is to use the recesses at one side of the chimney-breast and hide it behind full length doors, with a matching cupboard for clothes on the other side. Louvred doors are very useful in such situations as they allow for free ventilation of the air inside and for the steam to escape.

In a larger bedroom, particularly a long narrow one, you might well be able to achieve a separate dressing-room – something particularly worth aiming at if you dislike having the clutter of clothes and cosmetics in the bedroom itself. You may find you can build a bank of cupboards to partition off one end of the room and develop this space into a bathroom/dressing-room *en suite* with the bedroom. Again, there may not be room for a full-sized bath, but there should be room for a shower, basin and bidet.

If you make any additions to the plumbing of your house you will have to contact the health department of the local authority. If you find space to fit a new wc, the room that it is in must have a ventilated lobby, unless it opens directly into a bedroom and there is a second wc in the dwelling. So, for instance, if you make yourself a bathroom which includes a wc, out of a dressing-room opening directly from your bedroom, it must either have a ventilated landing, or, there must be another wc in the house. The entrance hall of a house, even if it does not have a separate window, is considered to be sufficiently ventilated by the opening and closing of the front door.

People often ask whether the wc should be in the bathroom or separate from it; the most workable rule is that, if there is only one wc in the house, it is most convenient if it is separate from the bathroom. If there are two wcs then it is a good idea to have one of these in the bathroom.

A workable bathroom can be much smaller than you think if you choose your fittings with care. A compartment only 5 feet by 2 feet 6 inches gives room for a wc, a sunken shower tray (fitted with wooden slats to make a continuous floor level) and, if you fit one of the new shallow basins such as Twyfords' 'Barbican' and 'Pramis', a basin as well.

Where space is short, you can either go for the wide, shallow basins or ones with more projection but with rounded-off corners and narrow rims. The wide, shallow ones achieve a standard-size bowl by putting soap trays to the side to reduce the depth front to back. Shires make the 'Ashby' 20 by 12 inches and 18 by 11 inches, incorporating a splashback. Johnson & Slater make the 'Murette' 23 by 12 inches and in three other smaller sizes; and Armitage's 'Dorex' is 23 by 12 inches and 20 by 12 inches. Of the round-corner basins, look at the CoID award-winning 'Sola' made by Twyfords, Ideal Standard's 'Roma', and any of the 'Lotus' range made by Adamsez.

Corner basins can sometimes help you out. Several are made which give the internal dimensions of a standard basin. These include Armitage's 'Corex' and Adamsez' 'Lotus' corner basin. Ideal Standard make the 'Anglesea', Johnson & Slater have their Y5016, and Shires make the 'Selby'. Most of these are available in smaller sizes for cloakrooms.

Although many of the basins suggested above can be carried by pedestals, cantilevered models take up the least space. You may be against these because you dislike the untidiness of exposed piping, but there is no longer any need for the ugly, old-fashioned trap. Several manufacturers make elegant chromium-plated bottle ones which fit snugly under the basin and can easily be unscrewed in the event of a blockage. There are plastic versions available which cost a lot less but some of these do tend to distort with heat and leak as a result. A compromise solution is Goslett's 'Mask' basin, which conceals the trap with a ceramic corbel set below to carry the basin.

The projection of wcs has reduced considerably. The Ideal Standard 'Lincoln' looks like any other low-lying suite but projects only 25 inches; Armitage make the 'Unitina' wash-down suite and the 'Unimyna' syphonic suite with the same projection. As a result of its $4\frac{1}{2}$-inch cistern, the Fordham Flush Panel suite projects only 23 inches and can be fitted where there was formerly a high-level wc installation without any alteration to the position of the soil waste-pipe, so that the cistern on its own can be used in conjunction with an existing wc where the high-level cistern only has failed, converting it to a low-lying suite. Where a syphonic pan is wanted, Armitage's 'Sylona' could be linked with the Fordham cistern still giving an overall projection of only 23 inches.

Where planning permits, another way of reducing the projection of the wc is to conceal the flushing cistern in a cupboard or duct in a room on the other side of the wall – it could be a bank of wardrobes or an airing cupboard. Both Fordham and Armitage make a plastic cistern especially for this purpose. Where you want to conceal the cistern in a panel or duct in this way, a wc which will fit absolutely flush against the wall, with no crevices behind to collect dust, is worth having. Goslett make the 'Chesta', Armitage the VC1206 and Twyfords the 'Clasp'. Because they give an uncluttered floor, the most space-saving of all are the cantilevered WCs. Some need to be bracketed into the back wall, others suspend from a cast-iron chair bracket, the base of which is sunk into the thickness of the floor. With both types, it presupposes that a certain amount of building work is going on. Where noise is a consideration, a syphonic WC is worth the additional cost as it is so much quieter in action.

The bidet is beginning to find greater acceptance in British bathrooms and most manufacturers include a matching one in their standard ranges. However, they are fairly elaborate pieces of plumbing equipment, which tends to make them expensive to buy and to install. Ideal Standard's 'Trimline' is the simplest version I know. It is really nothing more than a second wash-basin but oval-shaped and set at WC level. There is no central jet and water is simply introduced by two ordinary half-inch taps – you can match them with the others in your bathroom – and it is emptied by means of an ordinary plug. Bidets are also available wall-hung. Johnson Bros. make one; so do Armitage. This firm also makes the 'Oriana', a floor-standing model which is filled in at the back so that it fits flush against the wall or plumbing duct.

Where space is short, a low bath helps to make a small bathroom look larger, and good design can make a bath with an apparently short overall length more comfortable to use.

Although, because of its rounded bottom, the Allied 'Compac' is not so suitable for use with a shower, it gives generous inside dimensions of 4 feet 8 inches by 1 foot 10 inches, although it is only 5 feet by 2 feet 2 inches overall, as taps have been set at the corner, and rims at the side and end have been kept as narrow as possible.

If you want to incorporate a shower, choose a flat-based bath as wide as space will allow. Some short baths come in the standard 2 feet 4 inch width of the larger baths. Goslett do the widest I know, the 'Swanlyne' 2 feet 6 inches wide, and either 5 feet or 5 feet 6 inches long, with a square-ribbed base at the tap end and a substantial grab rail.

You can get a traditionally-shaped bath as little as 4 feet 6 inches long. However, where there is not room for even this, hip baths make a workable alternative, particularly if they are combined with a shower, and this is where the combination tap/showers such as the 'Mira' and Barking Brassware 'Hi-Lo' fittings are useful. The 'Mira' has a heat-control setting and there is the manually-controlled Barking Brassware 'Hi-Lo' and Bourners' 'Temperfix' range. Hip baths are ideal for bathing children and a lot of elderly people prefer them because they are easier to get in and out of.

Where space is very limited, showers are the answer and shower trays come in ceramic, Perspex and porcelain-enamelled cast-iron from 36 inches square down to 24 inches square. A shower soon pays for itself, as it uses about a fifth of the amount of hot water that a bath does, children find them more fun, and if you have a flexible pipe to the shower head and your basin is set close to the bath, it can be useful for hair-washing. If you consider fitting a shower, there are several points for which to look out.

First, it is essential that it incorporates some kind of heat control or thermostat so that there is no danger of scalding. Second, the cold water storage tank needs to be a minimum of 3 feet, but preferably more, above the operating height of the shower head, in order to give sufficient water pressure. If you are fitting a combined bath-tap/shower, this is essential. However, if you are fitting an independent shower, and it is not possible to achieve this head of water, Santon and Heatrae both make special valves which allow you to use cold water directly from the mains, combined with hot water from a storage cylinder. There are also two or three instantaneous electric water heaters run off the mains with shower heads which allow you to fit showers as high as or higher than the cold water storage tank.

Where an existing bedroom is being converted into a bathroom, you may find yourself with rather more space than you need. An over-large bathroom can often double as a dressing-room. It is a chance to create a luxurious retreat with a rest and exercise couch, a sun-lamp and basin set in a long well-lit dressing-table. A storage unit could make a useful screen and can be fitted with hanging space, shelves, drawers and flap-down sections as you need them. Continuous heating, even if only at a background level, and an extractor fan to pull out the steam will ensure that there is no damage to stored clothes.

Another solution is to let a too-large bathroom double as a laundry-room. This is especially worth considering if it is a second, perhaps children's, bathroom. With a washing-machine, tumbler-dryer and built-in linen and drying cupboards, the week's washing could be finished and aired and even ironed within an hour or so, leaving the kitchen free.

Where bathrooms are large, choose large handsome bathroom fittings; they will help to establish the right scale, and if you like coloured ware, this is undoubtedly when it is seen at its best. This gives you plenty of room for a bidet, and if the members of your family are tall, indulge in the luxury of a really long bath. They come as long as 6 feet 6 inches.

David Mlinaric, architect turned decorator, designed this bathroom for his own Chelsea flat. Here is an ingenious solution to the problem — common to many conversions — of where to put the bath, when space is tight. The basin is seen to the right, set against a completely glazed wall which doubles the sense of light and space

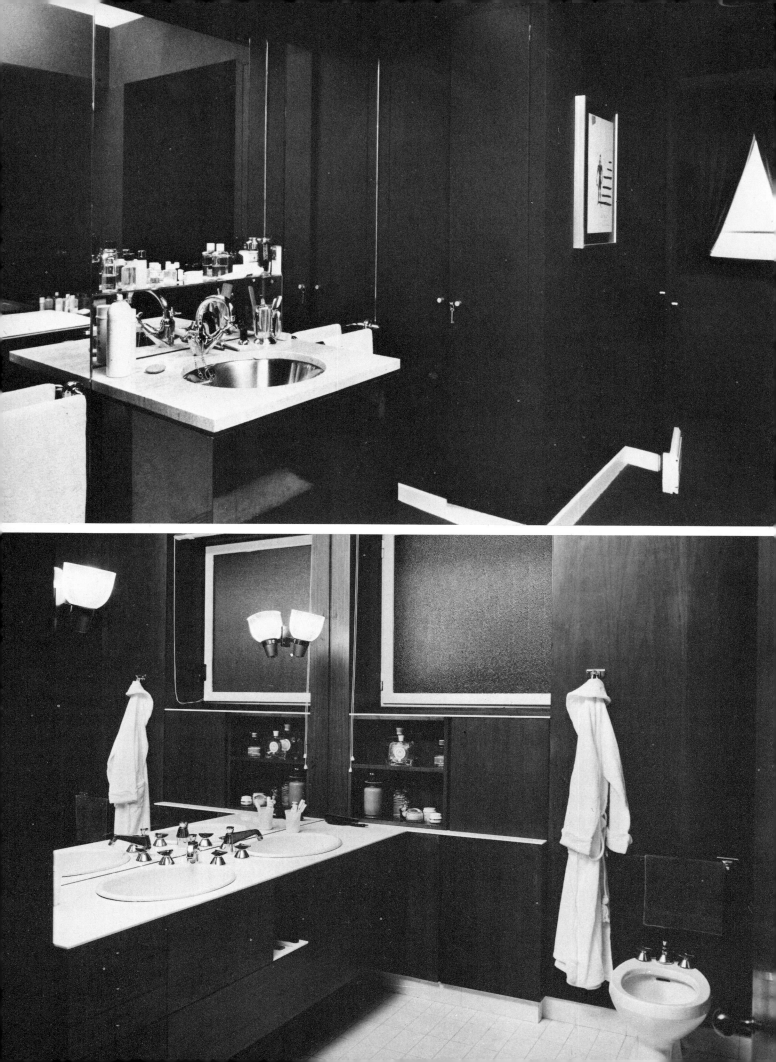

The use of dark finishes in bathrooms can be particularly successful, and makes an excellent contrast to white fitments.

Architect Anthony Cloughley demonstrates this in the bathroom from his own house shown opposite, above. The stainless steel circular basin set in a white marble top is housed in an alcove formed by the built-in cupboards. Dropped ceilings over the recesses serve to bring down the scale to one more sympathetic to low-level bathroom fittings. The mirrored wall behind basin and bath doubles the space of what is in fact a comparatively small room.

Walnut is used for both wall finishes and the handsome purpose-made unit in the Italian bathroom shown opposite, below. The two oval basins are set in a white marble slab. The wall above the basin is entirely mirrored.

In his own bathroom (right) architect David Rock has ingeniously overcome the limitations of the small floor area, finding room to incorporate not only a basin inset in a wide counter top but a bidet as well, and tucking the tap end of the bath under a storage cupboard. The floor covering runs up the side of the bath

Wall to wall mirrors can make a
bathroom seem twice as large. In
this example, designed by Angela
Connor, the other walls are panelled
in sealed pine boarding. Basin
lights are arranged like those in a
theatre dressing-room and the bath
is set centrally extended into a
marble bench seat

In this bathroom designed by
Anthony Cloughley the mirror runs
right up to the white ceiling so
effectively doubling its area. The
whole room is given an endless
note by the positioning of another
large mirror over the basin making
the reflections work in two directions

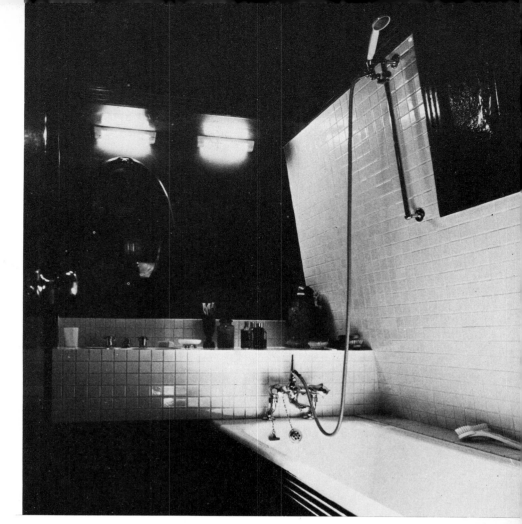

The use of an interesting texture in a bathroom — whether wood panelling, tiles or rough plaster — can add a touch of contrast, even drama.

The bathroom opposite opens off the master bedroom in an old Hampstead house and was designed by architect Edward Samuel. The louvred doors form part of a range which faces a bank of adjacent storage cupboards. Horizontal pine boarding lines the ceiling and walls. The white of the fittings is echoed in the background of the screen-printed floor tiles; the bath is half sunk in the floor.

High drama is the note of the tiny, mews house bathroom, above, by architect Max Clendinning. The mirror-like dark wall-finish sets off well the highly glazed, small white tiles which flank the bath and provide a handsome structural shelf. The tiles are barely two inches square and are closer to the rhythm and texture of mosaic than normal tiling.

The tiny bathroom (right) from a flat set amongst the rooftops of Bordeaux was designed by the owner, architect Patrick Fouquet. Centrally placed in the body of a house it is lit by an overhead skylight which further emphasizes the texture of its roughly plastered walls. These provide a rich contrast to the sleek surface of the black formica framing the fittings

UTILITY ROOMS

Town houses seldom have the sort of generous outbuildings or garages that can take the general overflow of household clutter in the way that houses in the country do, so when you start juggling with the space in your house, it is worth trying to find at least a corner that can be turned into a utility room/workshop. Its purpose and character will obviously vary with the space you can find for it and your family's needs. It could house a small bench for household tools and repair materials, as well as provide a place for cleaning equipment of every kind. Such a room can make a useful place for pets to sleep in and if it leads into the garden, it could provide an opening for a cat flap and so avoid draughts in a more vulnerable room. It could also house the central heating boiler, water softener, meters and a cupboard for bulk storage. It might operate as a laundry room, with a washing-machine, tumbler-drier, rack for airing and drying clothes, and ironing-board. Where it accommodates laundry equipment, it would be worth fitting a single sink with a draining-board so that washing done by hand can be done there and rinsed and spun in the machine. The sink and draining-board would then make it a useful place to arrange flowers, pot bulbs, wash Wellingtons, clean shoes, prepare animals' food and so on.

This leaves the kitchen free for its real job – food preparation and serving. If you divide the functions up in this way, you may well find you can do with a smaller kitchen than you had first envisaged.

If you can't find room for a separate utility room, but have managed to fit in two bathrooms or a downstairs cloakroom, you could try to make the second bathroom or cloakroom double as a laundry room. Alternatively, a small work bench with cupboards above and below might be fitted in a recess on a landing or under the slope of the stairs and screened with a curtain or folding sliding doors. Such a space under the stairs, particularly if adjacent to the kitchen could take a housewife's desk with space for cookery books, filing space for household accounts, guarantees, etc.

Large bathrooms and second bathrooms can often be designed to double as utility rooms.

The bathroom shown opposite, above was converted from an attic bedroom of an old house in Hampstead. The walls are lined with tongued-and-grooved boarding with a panel of Italian ceramic tiles set behind the bath. The WC is cunningly concealed in a recess behind the folding louvred doors, to the left. This arrangement would be equally useful to house washing machines and other laundry equipment when larger bathrooms do double duty as laundry rooms.

The handsome bathroom/utility room shown opposite, below, designed by Shirley Conran, has the bath neatly recessed in a wall of storage which incorporates, at the far end, an automatic washing machine with a tumble drier. Dark wall and floor surfaces contrast well with the white fittings. Two basins can be a great boon especially in family houses where things need to be speeded up in the morning. A drainage hole is set in the centre of the floor

EXTERIOR DECORATION

At last people have become aware of the fact that, in order to preserve the traditional (and inimitable) quality of our old towns and villages, we need to preserve groups of modest buildings every bit as much as the more impressive individual piles. And, where there are gaps and inconsistencies, exterior decoration can go a long way towards giving a street a sense of unity-within-diversity, as the Civic Trust schemes have so effectively demonstrated.

Happily, public spiritedness and self-interest can be combined, for the more sympathetically a house is related to its setting, the more attractive it is likely to be individually.

One difference between decorating the inside and the outside of your house is that, if your interior colour scheme proves disastrous, you alone will suffer, and, in any case, putting it right need not cost you too much. But if you misjudge badly on the colours you choose for the outside of your house, you are not only likely to dismay your neighbours but remedying it might well run to hundreds of pounds.

The other important difference is that, although thorough preparation is always the best policy, nothing very disastrous will happen if, in a quick bid to cheer things up, you give interior walls and woodwork a fresh coat of paint without bothering over much with preparing the surfaces. It may not last as long as it would if you had made a thorough job of it, but then you won't have done any positive damage. The outside of the house is a different matter. If the surfaces aren't well prepared and you don't choose the correct type of paint or finish, you'll end up, sooner rather than later, with rotten window frames that need renewing, rusty leaking down-pipes and gutters, and flaking wall surfaces.

Exterior decoration can be divided into three main sections: wall surfaces, woodwork and metalwork.

Wall surfaces

A sound principle with wall surfaces is never to rush into painting brick, stone or pebble-dash walls that have not been painted before,

The end elevation of this mid-Victorian corner house was in danger of collapsing outwards. To buttress it, architects Stout and Litchfield extended the porch up to the roof and down into the basement, and in the process gave the building a face-lift, modern in design but completely in scale and harmony with its neighbours however dreary they may look. If what prompts you is the need for protection against the weather, choose instead a colourless silicone water-proofer – far cheaper than paint, both to apply and to maintain. If it is looks you are concerned with, it is worth considering whether clever emphasis of the smaller elements could effectively distract the eye. Sharpened by a lot of white paint with a rich glowing colour for the front door, a dull, or even ugly, wall colour can often be transformed into an effective neutral foil. The colours and foliage patterns of climbing plants can also help a lot.

If you do decide to paint, however, and improvement in looks of the exterior of the house outweighs the arguments of trouble and expense of upkeep, then be sure to choose a permeable finish, that is, one that allows the walls to breathe. It will keep the rain out but will allow any water that has got into the wall to escape outwards.

Many of these finishes can be used equally satisfactorily over brick, stone, smooth plaster, pebble-dash or tile-hanging, which can be extremely useful if you need to simplify a fussy façade, but if you want to take in areas of mock half-timbering or weather-boarding, too, it is as well to check with the manufacturers whether the finish you have chosen is suitable for use on wood.

If the walls are already painted, then it is important to check carefully what sort of paint has been used. If they have been painted with an oil paint of an impermeable kind, you will have no alternative but to stick to this type of paint in subsequent redecoration.

If the paint used before is found to be water-based, an emulsion type can be used on top, provided the surface is thoroughly scrubbed down to remove any loose matter and treated with an appropriate sealant before repainting. But, whatever the existing surface and whatever the proposed treatment, it is important that it is absolutely free from loose particles (dirt, mould or lichen) and you should make this clear – in writing – when you instruct your decorator. Always specify the make and type of paint you want used, with the correct priming and undercoats, and that they are applied in strict accordance with the manufacturer's instructions. Paint firms will usually send their representative to advise you.

Where walls are in such a dilapidated condition that covering them is the only way to rescue the appearance of the house, there are several possibilities. If the bricks have spalled badly and the pointing has fallen away, you should have a good key for plastering. This might cost you no more than having the whole surface patched up and re-pointed, and it would certainly give the house better heat insulation. If the walls are to be plastered, insist that an appropriately soft plaster is used. Soft plaster is elastic and permeable and it won't crack and trap damp behind it.

If walls are in a bad state, particularly if you need insulation against cold as well as protection against rain, another solution is the traditional tile or slate hanging. These need no maintenance but you must be sure they are appropriate to the period and character of your house. The thick, textured finishes now available will also do a lot to unify and even up wall surfaces with a variety of textures – brick, stone, concrete blocks, etc – which are often found in a house with previous additions. But to get a consistent surface on a formal building, especially if the different materials appear on the same plane, it might be worth giving the walls a coat of soft plaster first.

A further wall surface that may well repay painting, even though it is in good condition, is the hard red Victorian brick you find in Midland towns, which wind and weather never seem to erode away. A coat of textured paint on this will considerably soften the house's character.

For lasting good looks, the choice of colour is as important as the type of finish. You need to bear in mind such things as the amount of dirt in the atmosphere and the amount of time and money you can afford to spend on upkeep. It is no good painting your town house white all over if you cannot afford to renew the paint for another six or seven years. It will look splendid for the first year or so, and then grow progressively more dismal and depressing. You would be better advised to paint the walls a rich, but more serviceable, colour such as an inky blue, dead green or dark ochre, terra cotta, earth brown; restrict your use of white to the frames and reveals of windows and doors, which are areas small enough to repaint at two- or three-yearly intervals.

It is sometimes difficult to know what to do about mouldings, particularly if they are excessively fussy, such as wedding-cake Edwardian. On a stucco house, these mouldings often look better painted in with the wall colour, with colour contrasts left to the windows and front door. Where mouldings are simple, some contrast with the wall colour can help to give clear definition to the house's features. Where the main wall area is unpainted brick or stone or a pale stucco colour, white provides the best contrast. Where the wall is painted a warmer colour, the alternative is to paint the mouldings a paler, cooler version of the wall tone.

Woodwork

The traditional way to protect woodwork is to paint it with a high-gloss paint using a lead-based primer if not a lead-based paint itself. Don't be tempted to use matt or semi-gloss paint outside; in fact, some manufacturers recommend one coat of undercoat and two of gloss for better protection rather than the more conventional two undercoats and one gloss.

In recent years, an alternative solution to painting and varnishing has appeared. There are now products called wood 'seals', frequently silicone-based, which unlike varnish (which provides a top skin), soak deep into the body of the wood. These can be clear or tinted, are easy and inexpensive to apply and maintain, and are particularly useful for garden structures. The Timber Research and Development Association will send you lists of proprietary makes.

If the woodwork is already painted, there is no real alternative but to continue to paint it. If the paint is a dark colour, it is wise to check whether it is bitumen-based. If so, and you propose to apply ordinary gloss paint (especially if it is a pale colour) over it, the bitumen in the old paint will tend to show through. However, this is no great problem as there are now proprietary sealers on the market which effectively prevent this happening. At the same time, it is possible to get bituminous paint in white and pastel colours.

With almost every wall colour, white is a good choice for door and window frames except for white-walled houses where black painted frames, if not sashes and casements as well, help to define the pattern that is made by the doors and windows on the façade.

The position of the front door should be made absolutely clear, so that it needs to be painted a colour which captures the attention. This need not be a bright colour, as it is more a question of contrasting tones – white or sharp pale grey against a warm red brick wall, for example, or burnt orange against cool grey stone. Garage and service doors, on the other hand, are better in blacks and greys or matched closely to the colours surrounding them.

Metalwork
Metalwork has to be painted with an oil-based paint. Any good quality exterior gloss paint is suitable and, in addition, there are several paints made specifically for use on metal. Again, as in the section on woodwork, check whether the old paint is a bitumen-based variety. Preparation of surfaces needs to be scrupulously careful so that all traces of rust are completely removed and any bare patches should be sealed with an appropriate sealer before repainting.

In most cases, gutters and down-pipes should be painted to blend with the colour of the walls: the less noticeable they are, the better. When they need replacing, choose one of the new plastic or glass-fibre varieties. The Building Centre will send you manufacturers' leaflets. These new rain-water systems are available in black, white and grey, round and square sectioned, are inexpensive, easy to fix and will never need repainting although, of course, they can be painted if it suits your scheme.

It is traditional to paint wrought-ironwork black or a very dark blue and cast-ironwork white; and again, as a general rule, it is difficult to improve on this.

Two successful restoration and conversion schemes are shown opposite; above, some 1811 houses at the Pierhead, Wapping, and below, an early nineteenth-century terrace in Islington. In both cases the buildings, rescued from a serious state of neglect, have been modernized and great attention has been paid to preserving the handsome proportions and balance of the terraces

THE GARDEN

However small and gloomy the patch behind your house is, don't despair. There is every chance that you can transform it into an enchanting vista to enjoy from the house and a leafy grotto to laze in on summer days. Where town gardens have such slummy surroundings or are so overlooked by neighbours that you are discouraged from using them, it is sometimes possible to give yourself privacy by extending the height of the walls with framing to carry climbing plants, and to add a pergola for protection from above. Trees, too, can help in this way. Marauding cats can be discouraged by chicken wire and Netlon as an alternative to trellis. But if you find you can't keep them out, there is an aerosol spray which discourages them from scratching up your most precious plants. Even if the garden remains one you prefer to look at, rather than to go out into, it is worth encouraging birds by providing them with plenty of cover, with food and water throughout the year.

Small gardens should be thought of as out-door rooms. As well as deciding what garden amenities you need, you will also have to take into account such unavoidable elements as tool sheds, dustbins, fuel stores, oil tanks and so on, all of which should be placed as unobtrusively as possible. If dustbins and fuel stores can be masked successfully in the front garden, or concealed in a front basement area, this is clearly the most convenient arrangement, as carrying dustbins and coal through the house should be avoided. Having a tank of oil at the back is another matter, as the pipe connection can still be at the front. You should use it deliberately as a vertical screening ingredient in your design, concealing it with a solid wall or light framework of trellis supporting a rampant evergreen such as the sweet-smelling Halliana.

Landscape designer John Brookes redesigned this Kensington garden to link through with the living-room of the house; thus the grey tiles in the house are echoed in the grey slabs of the terrace outside. The house is connected to the raised terrace under the tree by a white-painted pergola, the framing of which echoes that of the new sitting-room windows. The walls to the garden and an existing trellis were painted an ochre colour and are now covered with Russian vine. Pots, planted with annuals and bulbs, have been placed about the terrace, both inside and out. The overall effect is that the room is doubled physically, and certainly more than doubled visually, thanks to the interpenetrations of inside and out. This effect is strengthened by the windows not being curtained and the garden being lit at night

If you have small children, they will need space to pedal tricycles and push doll's prams around. A sandpit can be included, however limited the space, as it needn't be more than 2 feet square and it doesn't matter too much whether it is in sun or shade so long as it has a paved surround. Fill it with silver sand and give it a lid with a lip to keep out cats and rain.

You will need a place for sitting in the sun, having coffee, sometimes meals and even an occasional party. It's worth having at least one permanent bench or seat that can be left out in all weathers. What sort of design or material you choose should relate to the character of your house and the mood of your garden. It could be gothic-style wrought-iron or simply a slab of slate resting on a low brick plinth, exploiting a change of level. If you have room for a table, too, so much the better. So long as there is somewhere to sit, you will be tempted to wander out to snatch a few minutes of sunshine between chores. If you have to take a chair out as well, it becomes too much bother. If your garden is sunny and sheltered, and you like eating outside, you could have kitchen or dining-room chairs that could equally well be used out-doors, rather than finding storage space for special garden chairs. Wicker, rattan or bentwood arm-chairs would all do as they are light and easy to carry.

Such an area will need to be paved, as will any area immediately outside garden doors. When a garden is very small, you will make the space seem as large as possible by running paving across the whole area, leaving gaps here and there along the walls for planting. Avoid a rigid bed around the edges. It reduces the apparent size of the small garden as much as a border round a carpet does a small room. Under town conditions grass quickly gets worn and thin, especially if the area is intensively used. Changes of level, however, can suggest more rather than less space, and the colour and texture of paving, cobbles, gravel and chippings can add considerable colour and variety. You can select these in relation to the plants you are using with them and the nature of the garden itself, or you might extend the flooring of the house into the garden if it is an appropriate material. Pale paving reflects light back into the house, darker paving will absorb it but blue/black engineering bricks, for instance, can provide handsome contrasts with silver-leafed plants and other paving. You can sometimes get York and Portland stone paving slabs from your local council when they are taking up pavings, and marble and slate washstand tops can occasionally be rescued from junk yards. Where you can't find second-hand material and new stone will be too expensive, the new texture concrete paving slabs are far more sympathetic than the old type, giving a non-slip surface which allows moss and lichen to develop in the hollows, creating a more mature and natural look. Plants will soon start creeping over the edges to soften them.

Aspect and soil apart, it is terribly important to get full value back from every plant and shrub in a small garden. Check and re-check your list to see that you are getting scent (this can come from leaves as well as blossom), a long flowering season, leaves that look good most of the year round, either by remaining grey or evergreen or changing to brilliant autumn colours and, of course, berries. Concentrate first on creeping and climbing plants which will exploit the walls. Extend these with trellis if they are low, so that they drip with honeysuckle, jasmine, wisteria and roses to shut out the grime beyond. In this way, you will produce an atmosphere of luxuriant plant-growth without taking up too much of the precious ground-space. It may pay off to paint some of the walls white so that they can reflect back more light and heat. This can do a lot to offset the gloom where outside space is overshadowed for long periods. Pale pink, peach and ochre all look warm and make a marvellous foil for foliage. Entwined with leaves, large old mirrors too blotchy to use in the house can suggest mysterious and intriguing spaces beyond. If you are surrounded by very high walls, trailing tendrils and leaves over a pergola structure, either built out from the house or spanning the garden, can prevent the feeling that you are at the bottom of a deep well by stopping your eye at 8 or 9 feet above you instead of letting it slide up some 30 or 40 feet more to find a patch of sky.

In small gardens try to avoid too much contrasting flower colour. Use strong colour as an occasional high point. Whites and pastels will make the space seem larger, lighter and airier. Concentrate on the contrast of leaf shapes, textures and colours and on the forms of shrubs and plants. If you have a large tree that is blocking out light and draining the ground of nourishment, it may be better to have it out. This goes for any other tired plant or shrub that is not making a contribution. Because a garden is small, however, don't think that you must do without trees. There are plenty which never grow more than 15 feet high. You only need to be sure they are not placed where they will deprive you of sunlight.

Antique tanks and tubs can be expensive, but old yellow earthenware sinks rescued from houses under demolition make good alternatives. As well as leaving holes in paving for planting, one can often exploit changes in level or build them in, deliberately framing small raised beds with dwarf brick walls and perhaps extending these walls as plinths for seats.

Where you have a long narrow garden and are short of storage space for garden equipment and chairs, consider building a shallow summer-house/shed running along the entire width of the back wall. Imaginatively designed, it can provide a very pretty backdrop to your vista from the house. It could have a translucent or solid roof, but remember that you will be looking down on this from your upper rooms. Its front walls should be glazed at least above waist height, so that the eye penetrates through, and its back wall should then be painted white or a reflective colour. Again, its character should suit the mood of your house.

Water, particularly the sound of a fountain, can bring life and movement to the most unprepossessing patch of garden, but whether you install a fountain or not, do remember to allow for an outside tap of the kind that will take a hose connection. Remember, too, to install an outside power point. Lighting a garden is an excellent way of extending the apparent space of a house on summer evenings – even if it is too cold to sit outside.

A greenhouse or conservatory, will prove rewarding in many ways. If you enjoy gardening, you will find jobs to do the whole year round and, in winter, their shrubs and plants will help blot out the bleak winter scene beyond. Built on to the back or a side of a house, a conservatory can be warmed either by an extension of the main central heating system or by an independent heater. In any event, it usefully exploits heat-loss from the house and can feed back in the scent of flowers and leaves the year round.

If you want to plan the garden *and* do the work yourself, here are a few useful tips. First, measure the space and draw a plan. Note the height of surrounding walls and fences, the position and size of existing outhouses, paths and steps, as well as the larger shrubs and trees. With the last two, it is as well to find out their likely diameter and height when full grown, so that you can take this into account when you begin designing.

Find where the sun falls at different times of the day. You can do this by observation, remembering that the sun rises higher in the sky in summer, as well as having a wider swing than it does in the winter. Alternatively, you can use a child's pocket compass. This is vital information, as it will govern where you plan sitting-areas and what you will be able to grow. Although light is something you cannot add, you can reinforce what exists by reflecting it back with white walls, pale paving areas, white blossom, and mirrors, to the benefit not only of the plants but to the rooms inside the house as well. Also check the prevailing winds, taking into account that walls, fences, thick hedges and translucent screens can be used to shelter plants as well as people from cold northeast winds.

Before you select plants, you will need to know the character of the soil and what will grow in it. The survey, therefore, must include having this tested. You can buy a do-it-yourself kit or, for a full analysis of its components, you can send samples of the soil to your county horticultural officer. Members of the Royal Horticultural Society can obtain this service through the Society's gardens at Wisley. In all cases, you will not only receive an analysis but suggestions for providing a better balance.

Whatever the nature of the soil, you will find there is a group of plants which will positively enjoy what it has to offer. Don't grieve, for instance, because most rhododendrons and azaleas don't enjoy limey soil – lilac and clematis adore it.

Anyway, much can be done to extend the range of the things you can grow. Poor chalky soils can be enriched with acid-giving humus and artificial fertilizers (humus feeds the ground, artificial fertilizers the plant). If you live near a progressive sewage works, you may well be able to get a form of highly concentrated (and smell-free) organic manure. Heavy soils can be broken up and aerated by sharp silver sand; sour acid soils sweetened by lime; water-logged areas drained by ditches; and dry sandy soils kept moist and firm with rampant-growing, ground-cover plants. If you can afford it, you can always import a whole new layer of top-soil. In any event, you can make a pit with watertight sides and fill it with the mixture your favourite plant or shrub likes best. Providing there is the shelter and sun it needs, it will flourish there whatever the surrounding soil is like.

Gardening books and nurserymen's catalogues, give exhaustive lists of those plants which tolerate lime, need acid, sun, shade, well-drained ground or moist conditions, and so on. They vary within the groups to such an extent that one can't even say that all rhododendrons will fail on limey soil. Compare the catalogues and begin to assemble lists of possibilities. The most important thing is to have a garden which looks good the whole year round, so there is always something interesting to cut and bring into the house.

Follow up your survey by reading and taking any opportunity you can of visiting local private gardens, when they are open to the public. This will give you a chance to discover what grows really well in the district. You might even find a friendly head gardener to give you some tips. If there is a reliable nurseryman in the area, this is all to the good. He will understand local conditions and their problems, and his stock will be accustomed to them from the start. A further advantage is that anything you order won't have to spend days in goods vans and railway yards.

Although you'll want to start planning as soon as you take over the house, don't start making new paths, or do anything too radical, until you have given the garden a summer to show what it has already growing in it. Shrubs and trees are expensive, especially if they are of any size, and you may find you have some unusually interesting specimens lurking in the jungle.

Hold on to any materials, such as bricks from demolished out-houses, which might make paths or dwarf walls. Slabs of slate from old larder shelves can make all-weather table-tops or bench seats; glass can be used for cold-frames and so on.

Paved terraces and courtyards, skilfully laid, make an attractive extension to the living-area of the house and at the same time make the most, visually and practically, of the restricted space of the typical town garden.

The back garden of a terrace house in Kent, shown above, left, has been attractively paved and planted, and is linked to the ground-floor living-room by a flight of steps. To lighten the area the garden walls are painted a sandy colour.

Staggered paving stones, with the bits left in between attractively planted, can provide the answer to a small front garden, as shown above, right. Areas of loose pebbles or cobbles add textural contrast and interest.

Both these gardens were designed by John Brookes.

Small outside terraces can be formed around existing trees or plants to give them an established air, as was done by architect Robin Walker with the entrance patios of his single-storey courtyard house in Dublin shown below, left. Every room of the house looks out on to a plant-filled court-yard, and cross vistas are opened up through the linking of inside and outside spaces.

A well-paved terrace can be used as an extension to the inside of the house as with the conversion, by architects Stout and Litchfield shown below, right, where the basement dining-room opens directly onto the paved garden where meals can be served in fine weather

If you find a long-established lilac or rhododendron plumb in the middle of the one space that would give you a sheltered sitting area, don't have any scruples – have it out. On the other hand, the existing trees and shrubs may well provide you with guide lines for your future layout, the focal point of a vista, or screening for the inevitably untidy sandpit and play area.

Once you have discovered what plants are there, and which ones you want to keep, find out what kind of treatment they need: when they require pruning, whether they need cutting back, how to keep them longest in blossom and so on. You may well find that this has been neglected for years and the stock is better than it appears. In the same way, the soil may have been starved of nourishment.

Professional help

Landscape architects are not only useful for large-scale work at stately homes and municipal gardens. They are well worth consulting if you want to get the most out of a small plot. They are more reliable than many landscaping contractors, who will unblushingly recommend Cotswold stone for rockeries and dwarf walls in the heart of London; they will cost you no more either, as the contractor will have allowed for a design fee, albeit invisible, in his quotation for the work.

The landscape architect makes a survey of the garden, noting the character and position of any features – paths, walls, and so on – and the condition and probable life of the shrubs and trees. On the basis of this raw material, he will design the lay-out and planting to meet any special needs of the client – a lily pool, for example, a greenhouse or a children's play area – always bearing in mind the time and labour available for the upkeep of the garden.

When you have approved his scheme, the landscape architect draws up detailed drawings and specifications which he sends out to two or three gardening contractors for competitive estimates. The contractor is chosen on the basis of price and competence. The landscape architect then supervises the job until completion.

In general, he charges in the following way: on a time basis – a minimum of £3·50 an hour rising to £6 or more, plus expenses; work over £2,000 – on a percentage basis.

As a member of a professional institute, a landscape architect cannot advertise. You might find one by seeing his work featured in a magazine or book on gardens, or from personal recommendations. An architect friend might well suggest some names. Otherwise, write to the Institute of Landscape Architects.

If, however, you want to do the work yourself, a landscape architect should supply you with a master plan and all the necessary information on planting, etc, and would be available for advice.

The Cambridge garden shown here is a typical town plot, only 19 feet by 40 feet, but these restricted dimensions were exploited by the owner, architect Nathan Silver to make a garden which is full of visual interest yet demands little maintenance.

Originally, it was accessible from the garage or a steep basement stairway, but as the basement and first floor of the house were to become dining-room and sitting-room, and old concreted yard and two sheds were removed and half the area was excavated to form a stepped brick terrace. In this way, more light reaches the basement dining-room, and the terracing rises via a redwood stair, along the east wall, up to the living-room. The stair itself forms the hinged lid of a storage unit for garden tools. The brick terracing goes up in 6-inch and 18-inch steps, making interesting visual changes of level and informal seating. There is also a built-in charcoal grill for barbecues, and the whole garden is spotlighted

Where a particularly fine tree is already growing it can often be used as the pivot around which the garden is designed. Added emphasis can be provided by a bench surround, or by concentric paving, as illustrated in the two examples shown here, one with an ancient plane tree, the other with a magnificent catalpa.

Keith Lacey designed the Cadogan Place garden shown above. It was heavily shaded by a magnificent plane tree, and as the more light one can get into a garden the better the plants will grow, some of its lower branches were removed and a seat built round its trunk. As lawn wears so badly, particularly in town gardens, paving was laid

instead. The attractive use of trelliswork to embellish the wall and door adds depth, making the garden area appear larger than it is.

Beautifully laid paving and a fine old catalpa are features of the Kensington garden, shown opposite, designed by Ian Mylles. It is 56 feet long by 34 feet wide, sheltered from the north by the house and contained on the other three sides by 4-foot high brick walls. Before it was redesigned the garden consisted of a small neglected lawn, with narrow borders almost devoid of plants, on three sides, and some very poor paving; this was replaced with Old York paving laid in a rectangular pattern with granite setts for contrast

THE STRUCTURE

Major planning changes apart, it is the way you deal with the structural details and finishes that will most affect the character of the house. Unless the architectural elements are right, however compelling the subsequent decoration, you won't achieve a satisfying result. This section deals with the structural details and surface treatments of a building – doors, windows, floor and wall surfaces, fireplaces, storage. None of these elements can be considered in isolation but must be related in your thinking, right from the beginning, with the sort of design character you want to achieve. Thinking through this stage demands a lot of discipline as you may have to be prepared to discard individual cherished dreams for the good of the whole. How you treat the structure may be decided to some extent for you by its present condition. Where a house has most of its windows and interior mouldings, doors, fireplaces and so on, in a reasonable state of repair, there is an argument for maintaining the existing character and matching it through in any new work you may need to do. Certainly, if you want to keep costs down, yet push up the house's market value, it is worth retaining and reinforcing its existing period character. But if you do this, aim at authenticity and resist decorators repro.

If you want to break down the existing structural character in a drastic way, and the property is in a poor state of repair or its existing character negligible, then there is a good case for remaking it in completely modern terms.

Walls and wall finishes

Walls, ceilings and floors define the spaces in which we live. These seemingly solid barriers are less rigid than they appear. Paint them white, they recede; paint them bright red, they approach; paint them dark green and they melt into shadows. Large mirrors play similar tricks, making you feel there is twice as much space and light. High-silled windows make a small room become a box, but light streaming through a wall at floor level from a french door and linking the floor with a terrace outside will make the floor seem larger.

Obviously no one can make a small-roomed house seem a mansion, but there are ways of deceiving the eye so that spaces seem other than what they really are. It may even be that you want less space visually, not more. You may have overwhelmingly large Edwardian rooms that you wish to make more cosy, or rooms that are at present dull and box-like which you want to turn into something more workable. Many of the answers to these problems lie in the way the wall surfaces and ceilings are treated.

Wall finishes: Wall coverings have three functions. First, they should provide an easily maintained surface, bearing in mind the purpose of the room. Second, by colour, texture, scale and general character they should contribute to the atmosphere within the room itself. Third, they should also be an insulation barrier against heat loss. Tapestries and wood panelling have always had a practical, as well as decorative, purpose.

In older houses dampness is usually the first problem to solve. Until walls are dry, or the dampness is at least shut off from the interior of the house, they will remain cold and subject to condensation, thus remaining a threat to any sub-

Even when a building is as neglected and decayed as the one shown opposite, technical know-how and modern treatments can save it and adapt it to present-day standards of comfort and convenience

sequent decoration. Damp-proofing in connexion with walls is discussed fairly fully in the section on *Basements*. It is re-assuring to know that there are now several reliable professional methods of treating rising damp in walls and for information on these you should contact the nearest Building Centre.

Where there is also the problem of rain penetration, you will need to provide vertical protection as well. It is now considered preferable to waterproof the inner face of the wall rather than the outer one as, once an impervious finish on the other face cracks, any water getting behind it is trapped. This doesn't apply, of course, if you use slate or tile hanging as air can move freely under these.

If the plaster-work is in very bad condition, this may be because the wall itself is damp, or it may be that rooms have been left unventilated or unheated for so long that the deterioration is simply the result of condensation. There are two possible solutions – to strip off the plaster and re-plaster the wall, or to fix battens and panel the walls in some way. Where the walls are damp because of rain penetration, you can apply Newtonite to the stripped wall. This is a corrugated bituminous felt which acts as a damp-proof membrane, a key for the plaster and, by vitue of its vertical corrugation, allows for ventilation of the wall fabric. These air pockets also serve to provide insulation. This is better than the more common method of brushing the stripped brick with a bituminous compound, and then plastering directly onto it as, unless an insulating vermiculite plaster is used, the internal walls surface will continue to be cold from the dampness of the wall on the other side of the bituminous skin.

Where the trouble is not damp penetration from the outside, but simply condensation on a cold wall, the alternative is to use a dry lining – plasterboard – that either incorporates a backing of glass fibre or aluminium foil. This will add noticeably to the insulation of the walls and, as it only needs a skim coat to finish it, will reduce the drying-out period considerably. It may be necessary with old walls to attach these plasterboard panels with a framework of battens. Where the wall face is fairly even, dabs of plaster may be sufficient.

Battens can support a variety of other wall finishes: tongued-and-grooved boarding, ply with veneer face, 'Glinex' (an attractive honey-coloured linen fibre board), panels of cork, etc. All these materials provide a rich, permanent finish which, in itself, gives excellent insulation. This can be even further improved by hanging aluminium foil behind the battens or filling the spaces between with mineral wool.

When using rigid panels, it is important to work out an effective pattern of joints which relate to the architectural elements of the room. The manufacturers of the different boards will send you pamphlets suggesting various methods of jointing. The advantage of using tongued-and-grooved boarding is that it will successfully adapt to old houses in which walls, ceiling and floors are out of true, whereas the rigid rectangle of a panel material can make these faults

more apparent. Tongued-and-grooved boarding can be used equally well set vertically, horizontally or diagonally and can be simply sealed with a polyurethane seal or painted.

Where there are plaster walls that you want to paint or paper, the smoother the surface, the better. Where plaster is simply fragile, a smooth-faced, linen-backed lining paper will hold it together. Where it is bumpy, it should be rubbed down first to get rid of projections. Then, if you want to paint the walls, there are textured lining papers that you can use as a base. These range from simple wood chip to the sturdy Lincrusta papers so beloved by the Victorians. Sandersons carry several good ones. Or you can stick hessian to the wall and paint over that. Where very tough washable surfaces are needed, undoubtedly the higher the glaze the longer the life, but, with bumpy walls, a high gloss does highlight the irregularity of the surface.

You may find, of course, that the colour you want is already available in one of the textured wall fabrics or vinyl-faced papers. These range from coarse linen, grass cloth, and fine silk to the sturdy plastic finishes, such as Vymura.

Pattern is another way of disguising bumpy wall surfaces. Here, the important thing is to choose a pattern that is appropriate to the scale of the room. A number of wallpapers are themselves washable, but if you find one you like which isn't already treated, this can be done on all but the flock type.

Where walls are dry, lino and vinyl sheeting can be fixed to the plaster with a standard flooring adhesive. This gives a tough surface that is heat insulating and not as noisy as a tiled one. It can be very useful in bathrooms, kitchens and children's rooms. Flooring tiles of all kinds can be used in the same way. Cork is particularly handsome when used on walls and is worth considering in a room where you have hi-fi equipment or play any kind of musical instrument.

Texture, pattern, scale and character all have to be taken into account when choosing wall finishes. Texture is useful quite apart from its ability to disguise bumpy plaster, as it can contribute a sense of richness and luxury to rooms whether it is used in conjunction with neutral or positive colour.

Big rooms can take high ceilings, unless that is, the furniture is so small in scale or so low-lying that the high ceiling dwarfs it. Some Victorian and Edwardian houses are especially awkward as they have very high ceilings although the rooms themselves are small. Dropping the ceiling physically is obviously one way of dealing with this but it is an expensive job, and the height of the window head may make it impossible. However, painting a ceiling in a rich or dark colour can effectively reduce its apparent height – even more so if the ceiling colour is brought down to the bottom of the cornice. Where there is no cornice, take the ceiling colour down to the picture rail. If the room is too dark to take a light-absorbing ceiling, the ceiling can remain white and the walls given a strong horizontal emphasis. This will also have the effect of lowering the room and could be horizontal boarding or striped or patterned wallpaper hung lengthwise. If the room has a dado, paint it to contrast with the wall treatment above.

In such rooms, bookshelves should be kept as low as possible, not rising higher than the head of the door frame, and the horizontal lines of the shelves should dominate the vertical supports. Pictures, however enormous, should be hung at eye level, and small pictures will look best if grouped in horizontal blocks.

Where ceilings are low, the reverse principles apply. Paint the ceiling, cornice and moulding white; strip off existing picture rails and carry the wall finish right up from skirting to cornice or ceiling. If the room has a dado, paint wall and dado as one, or the dado to match exactly the background colour of the paper above. Choose wall finishes with a vertical emphasis – vertical boarding, stripes and patterns. Take bookshelves from floor to ceiling and let the vertical supports predominate. Flood light on to the ceiling, but don't fix a light on it. Here pictures should be grouped vertically if they are small, and large pictures avoided altogether.

Strong contrasts break a room up into its various elements and thus make it seem smaller. This can work usefully to articulate large rooms, but in small rooms it can seem restless. The aim here should be to unify the decoration. You can match wallpaper and curtain fabric so that a continuous pattern runs around the room. If the paper is a non-directional one, it can be run over the ceiling as well. Paintwork should pick up the background colour of the pattern. Walls and woodwork painted white make any room seem larger and a mirror can extent this illusion even more effectively. In a small room which you want to look particularly rich, as well as larger, you could try one of the shimmering silver and gold papers which are now available. They look particularly magical at night, as the plane and limit of the wall are elusive and difficult to define.

The scale of a wallpaper pattern – that is, its size in relation to the size of the wall – is extremely important. In a small room, a large-scale pattern is overwhelming unless the room almost totally lacks furniture and other decoration, and even then it will decidedly reduce its apparent size. For this reason, a large-scale pattern is useful when you wish to make an extra large room seem smaller and more friendly. Generally if you wish to use a patterned finish in a small room, keep it small and not too overpowering.

When you are converting something like a warehouse, exploiting cellar or attic space, or building new walls as a part of an extension, it may be possible to leave the brickwork or stonework unpainted; wirebrushing old walls will often remove a surprising amount of dirt to bring up some good colour underneath. Where this treatment would give too dark a finish, or the surface is not suitable, a handsome effect can be achieved by painting with one of the textured finishes commonly used for external decoration such as Snowcem or Sandtex. A hard plaster with a smooth finish can make such simple spaces seem bleak and austere.

Care of floors

If you want floor finishes that wear well, look good and feel comfortable, the base you lay them on needs to be dry, insulated and levelled. Damp floors are unhealthy as well as damaging to floor-coverings and decoration. Uninsulated floors present a large area through which heat can escape from the house, a fact which is often overlooked; and uneven floors result in finishes giving half the wear they might have done.

Dampness is often a problem in a basement or, where there is no basement, in the ground floors of old houses where stone, brick or even concrete floors were laid without a damp-proof course.

If the stone slabs or bricks are particularly handsome and worth retaining, you can lift them, lay a concrete slab plus damp-proof course, and then re-lay them in a cement screed, pointing up with matching mortar.

If you don't want to retain the old floor and the room can afford to lose an inch or so of ceiling height, run a 2-inch screed over the top of a bituminous damp-proof membrane. A new finish can then be laid on this.

You can lay quarry or any other clay tiles directly onto a slightly damp concrete floor so long as they are bedded in a waterproof cement. For lino and vinyl sheet flooring or carpet, brush the slab first with one of the new polyurethane damp-proofers, such as Supaseal and top this with a thin levelling screed.

With any of the previous treatments, the damp will have been checked but the surface will still be cold and, where this will matter, cork, woodblock or a foam or felt-back sheet finish would be a good choice. If you are laying carpet, use a thick rubber foam underlay. Unfortunately, you cannot rely on this to double as a damp-check as it is porous.

In old houses you will frequently find suspended timber floors on the ground floor or basement. If you lift a board you will probably find earth beneath and no protective concrete slab. Where this is the case, it is particularly important that you check that the airbricks providing underfloor ventilation are kept free. Once blocked, the damp, still air will quickly encourage dry rot. Even where a timber floor of this kind is in good condition, and the ventilation obviously effective, it is still a mistake to cover its entire surface with some non-porous material like lino. Restrict this sort of finish to small areas such as kitchens and cloakrooms where it is essential, and leave the rest of the boards polished or covered with rugs or matting. Where such timber floors show much evidence of rot, it is worth facing the upheaval of stripping them out and laying a new concrete floor with damp-proof course.

When laying new floors, take the opportunity to build in as much insulation as possible. Polystyrene foam panels or mineral quilt can be laid on top of the concrete ground slab before the cement topping screed is laid, as a buffer against heat loss. Alternatively, or even additionally, the screed itself can have vermiculite mixed into it to improve its insulating qualities.

Before you rush to cover old board on upper floors, remember that they may well provide a floor finish in themselves. Sanding can often reveal lovely honey colours in the saddest-looking old boards. Left unstained and sealed with a polyurethane finish, such as Bourne Isate or Kingston's Translac, they will have a tough finish that will last for years and never need polishing. But warn the plumber and electrician not to savage them when they are installing new pipes and cables. Where boards are sound, but too stained for sanding, they can be painted. Kingston make a polyurethane floor paint which can also be used to refurbish old lino and tiles should you find some laid in good condition but the wrong colour. If you find the range of colours rather limited experimental blending will produce some pleasant sludgy-browns and inky-blues. If the boards are really too battered to rescue, an effective and inexpensive answer is to cover them with $\frac{1}{4}$-inch birch-faced ply. This comes in 2 foot square panels which you simply pin down with panel pins at the corners and the middle of each edge. Loose nails should be knocked into the boards and serious unevenness planed off first and the panels laid on a felt paper underlay. Even cheaper still – and a particularly good solution for children's rooms – is to lay hardboard, smooth side upwards and sealed. It develops an attractive rich brown colour and makes a useful first stage base on which you can lay grander finishes later.

One of the easiest finishes to lay is Lynx interlocking ply parquet, which you build up to form one large sheet. It is not pinned down and so can be taken away with you when you move. Other forms of ply parquet are pinned down at the corners in the same way as the ply panels described above.

If you want to lay sheet or tile lino, plastic or cork floorings on floorboards, it is essential to lay gaboon resin-boarded plywood first; even if the boards are level, their edges will show through in time. Hard tiles can be laid on wooden floors but a really rigid base is essential to avoid the joints cracking, so if you want to do this, it means bringing in a specialist firm. However, some ceramic and mosaic tiles can be laid on wooden floors in a flexible latex base.

If floor finishes are to look good, they must also be tough enough to withstand the wear they are given. So you need to consider carefully the conditions they will be used under, whether the floor will be a good insulator against cold and noise, have to take daily mopping, occasional spills, children's gumboots or be pleasant to walk on in bare feet.

Your last concern is which colour, texture, scale or pattern of treatment generally is going to do most for the spaces. If your house is small, or if you are converting it into separate flats, it is particularly worth trying to keep continuity in the colours, if not the materials, of the floor finishes. Matching the tiles you use in the kitchen and bathroom with the colour you are using for the carpet in hall, living-room and bedrooms, will help to link the small spaces of individual rooms into one larger seeming space.

Even if your house is large enough to stand markedly different floor treatments in each room, it is important that when you move around, or when doors are left open, there is a pleasant relationship between the floor finishes.

If you have oddly-shaped rooms with a great many projections, a plain or mottled finish is the one to choose: definite patterns accentuate irregular shapes. Some degree of pattern or gentle mottling is easier on floors which have heavy use and daily marking. Large spaces, particularly those that are rather empty of furniture (such as halls) can be made to look more finished with a handsome geometrically-patterned floor and stripes can be set across the width of a long room or passage to make it appear wider and shorter.

Variations in floor finish make any room look smaller, but are useful in large multi-purpose rooms in which they help to define the different areas. You might choose blue-black quarry tiles in the kitchen section, cork tiles for the dining-area and cork tiles covered with a big fur rug where you sit.

The tile size plays an important part. Small tiles suit small spaces, large tiles greater spaces. If you have large rooms a pleasant floor finish is obtained using 12 inch square tiles. I like tiles set diagonally to the walls, rather than parallel: the result is less rigid and has a wall-spreading effect, it is useful too as it disguises the fact that walls that should be parallel, are not – frequently the case in old and not-so-old houses.

Before deciding on a patterned carpet, remember that it will govern your choice of wallpapers, curtains and upholstery for years to come: and date the room more seriously than any other factor. If wear and possible marking are important considerations, a curly textured, very small geometric or very finely-stripped finish would leave more scope for future schemes.

Where you want to give an impression of more light and space, pale-coloured floors are best. Warm colours bring warmer light into cold, north-facing rooms; neutral colours – and this extends to muted blues, browns, and greens – are a good choice for general-purpose rooms, such as family living-rooms and bed-sitting-rooms, which house a great variety of activities and possessions. Where existing walls, curtains and furniture are pale in colour and the ceiling high, a fairly deep-toned floor can help stabilize the scheme.

If you live in a town and miss having shrubs and trees around, browny green floor backed by potted plants and plenty of white can create a pleasant illusion of grass and green shrubs just outside the door. If your sitting-room opens on to a terrace paved with brilliant terracotta tiles, avoid the clash of a bright pink carpet; choose a colour that marries in or complements the tile colour. Or if you have bright red brick houses opposite and they are fairly close and always in the line of vision, choose a floor colour that won't conflict violently with the red brick. Otherwise, you will have a persistently jarring note in the room.

Sound insulation

We are constantly under attack from noise, both from without and within. Noise from outside is mainly airborne – the sort that comes from passing traffic, nearby schools and factories, railways and aeroplanes. This penetrates mostly through windows and doors; walls by comparison are pretty efficient sound barriers.

So, the first step is to draughtstrip your windows and doors thoroughly. Where the trouble is serious, the next step is to double-glaze windows (see page 204). To be effective there should be at least 4 inches between the two frames, though 8 or 10 is even better, if the thickness of the wall will allow. For best results, you should go to a double-glazing firm which specializes in this. The Insulation Glazing Association will give you names. Similarly, a second door in the hall not only gives you a draught lobby but helps to keep traffic noise out.

Trees and shrubs will, to some extent, absorb airborne noises, but they need to be planted pretty thickly to provide an effective barrier and, of course, they need to be evergreen to be useful the whole year round.

Unless you live near an aerodrome, there is little need to insulate the roof-space against noise penetration, although you should do it anyway to prevent heat loss. The problem is to seal all the cracks, but, if you pack to the top of the joists with loose fill and lay 2 inch polystyrene sheeting over them, it can make quite a difference.

If you seal up the house against noise, however, you will have to provide some sort of assisted ventilation, unless one side of the house is much quieter than the other and you can ventilate it satisfactorily from there. You can get advice about mechanical ventilation both from the London Heating Centre and the Electricity Council. Mechanical ventilation need not necessarily mean ducted air conditioning linked with a warm air heating system. There are a number of very quiet individual room ventilators on the market, which can be inserted through an external wall.

You may, of course, be troubled through structure-borne noise from your neighbour's house or flat and, if this is the case, it is no good hoping to cure it by putting insulation on your side of the wall or floor. If friendly overtures don't succeed in persuading them to move their television set, or whatever is causing the nuisance, to the other side of the room or to another room altogether, the simplest solution is to build wall-to-wall cupboards (keep them as full as possible) or hang bookshelves on the shared wall to provide an additional barrier to the sound. The professional way of treating such problems is to provide a special structural skin over the entire wall or the floor through which the noise is penetrating. If the noise problem is acute, it is worth asking an architect to design such a skin for you and to supervise the installation. The work in itself won't cost very much but the know-how of its construction is usually outside the average small builder's experience.

Inside the house the way to stop noise transmission is to deal with it at source. Typewriters, sewing-machines, radios, record players, televisions, etc, can be set on rubber pads. Other equipment should be chosen for its low noise level, so long as its efficiency isn't materially impaired. *Which?* magazine frequently gives the comparative noisiness of equipment in performance tests, and you can always ask to hear equipment working before purchasing it.

Unless you have silent models, avoid setting refrigerators and other electrical equipment against thin partition walls. it is worth noting that solid brick internal walls transmit sound less than stud ones (timber-framed). You can tell which is which by knocking them – the stud ones sound much more hollow. Thin partitions act as amplifiers of noise conveyed through the pipes or sanitary fittings fixed to them, so, where possible, fit these to the thicker outer walls, or ensure that the fitting itself is insulated from the partition.

If your plumbing is seriously noisy, call in a good plumber to check it. You can however, lessen the hiss of water running through ball valves during the refilling of a cistern or tank by fitting the valve with an extension pipe which discharges under water so that the sound is not free to radiate into the air, and the noise of flushing can be reduced considerably by using a syphonic pan and a good low-level flushing system.

Once you have insured that home equipment makes as little noise as possible, you can take the edge off this even further by finishing and furnishing the rooms with the most sound-absorbent materials suitable. This reduces the transmission of noise to other parts of the house and certainly does something to reduce airborne noise that penetrates from outside. Clearly, where it is possible, the ideal solution is to have thick-lined and interlined curtains, wall-to-wall carpet with a thick form underlay, generous upholstery, plenty of cushions and an absorbent wall finish, such as fabric or cork.

Where the prevention of noise penetration is very important, such as for a study used by someone working at home all day, internal doors can be draught-stripped and given a flexible threshold. If doors seem very flimsy, panels can be usefully filled with fibre-board on both sides and faced with plywood. A most successful sound deadener is to line the walls with ½-inch or 1-inch thick cork boards. These were originally used for packing but have now become popular as an insulating wall finish. The London Building Centre, will give you the names of firms who make it, or you can get it ½-inch thick from Habitat Designs Limited, PO Box No 2, Wallingford, Berkshire. This material is very useful in children's rooms, where inevitably there will be less possibility of soft furnishing, as it makes an excellent pin-up board. Foam or felt-backed lino, vinyl sheet or sealed cork can all take some of the impact noise out of children's floors. Laying fibre-board below this would help even more and is a useful solution when rooms are used for, say, music practice. In children's rooms wicker, cane and bentwood furniture is useful as it doesn't make as much noise when it is pushed around or knocked over as heavier wooden pieces do. Ceilings, too, can be lined usefully with any sort of insulation board or tiles, but check first that they are not inflammable and that their effectiveness is not reduced by painting them.

Kitchens, too, are clattery places. They can be given the same sorts of floors as suggested above for nurseries. Ceramic tiles can look wonderful, but lining the walls with cork, lino or vinyl, in sheet or tile form, will not only make for quieter conditions but prevent condensation. Wooden fittings make less noise in use than do metal ones, and plastic-covered equipment is the quietest of all. The best quality lino makes an excellent working surface as it absorbs noise.

Wet and dry rot

Wet rot, dry rot and various beetles can produce such alarming manifestations that many people will dismiss a house which is in every other way suitable. What they don't realize is that it is now possible to deal with all three quickly, effectively and at a very reasonable cost.

It is no good attempting to deal with rot until you have dealt with damp in all its forms, as it is damp that produces both wet and dry rot. Dampness in houses can be caused in the following ways, and it is advisable to check each one in turn.

Rain penetration: this can be dealt with externally by tile or slate hanging, weather-boarding, colourless silicone water-proofers or emulsion finishes that allow the wall to breathe, never an impervious finish, such as gloss paint or plaster, which seals the damp in. Alternatively, you can line the walls with a waterproof key for plaster, such as Newtonite, or brush the inner faces with a waterproofing compound, such as Synthapruf.

Rising damp: this can be dealt with by any of the internal lining methods mentioned above, or by an electro-osmosis installation, by silicone latex injection, or ventilating tubes set at some 6 to 9 inches above ground level.

Rising damp in floors: it can be treated either by building in a structural damp-proof course or by laying thick polystyrene sheeting underneath the floor-covering.

Structural defects: gutters and downpipes can rust at the back, letting water soak into the walls unnoticed. Missing tiles and slates will allow rain to get in or snow to drift under. Pointing in the joints of brickwork and at junctions of roof, as well as the flashings of chimneys, all need to be kept in order – otherwise these will provide paths for rain.

Condensation: this is a cause of dampness that is often neglected. Basically, it is the moisture in the air condensing on the walls because they are cold, but it can be severe enough to destroy decoration, even causing wallpaper to peel and fall from the walls. The cure is ventilation and warmth. Ventilation is also essential beneath suspended timber ground floors, so keep air bricks clear, thus enabling air to circulate, and keep the timber dry to prevent dry rot from setting in.

The Noise Abatement Society, which was responsible for getting the Noise Abatement Act through Parliament in 1960, has risen out of a widely-felt need for protection against the alarming increase in noise. Anyone who is troubled by noise in any form would find membership a good investment. This entitles you to information and reports on noise abatement topics. The Society will also give members advice on any specific technical or legal problems, and help from its panel of experts is available at special rates. In addition, for a small subscription fee, you can get a monthly digest which gives examples of situations where noise reduction has been effectively achieved. Anyone interested further in this subject should purchase the Law Society Stationers' *Law and Noise*.

Wet rot occurs where wood is pretty continuously soaked with water but enjoys a reasonable air circulation around it. Once the cause of dampness is cured, wet rot goes. However, it is important to remove any decayed wood and treat the surrounding area, as the drying-out can provide any dry rot spores that may be present with perfect conditions in which to geminate. You can recognize wet rot fungus by the long fine strands of fungus it forms. The timber tends to crack along its length and darken.

Dry rot occurs when timber is continually or periodically damp, and where the air is still. This is why it is so frequently found in the joists of suspended ground floors when air-bricks which should be ventilating the underfloor space have become blocked up.

Dry rot produces warping and shrinkage and is recognizable by a musty, mushroomy smell. Timber cracks into squares and develops an orange to deep brown-coloured fungus. Before it has reached this state, the timber will have begun to disintergrate, and it is possible to tell whether rot or worm is present by prodding with a sharp, pointed penknife. Where it is decayed, it will go in easily.

Rot is a serious business. It can destroy the main timbers of the building surprisingly quickly, and for this reason there is everything to be said for going to a firm which specializes in treating it so that they can identify the type and cure the cause of damp effectively, eradicate the rot and treat the surrounding area to prevent its reappearance. If you have only a small outbreak which you feel your builder could tackle, I recommend you send for the *Wood Preservation Leaflet No 1*, issued by the British Wood Preserving Association, which deals with the causes, remedy and prevention of wet and dry rot, and the *Forest Products Research Laboratory Leaflet No 6: 'Dry Rot in Building – Recognition, Prevention and Cure'*. You should insist that your builder carries out the instructions contained in them, and that he carries out the manufacturers' instructions for any fungicide that is used. *The Wood Preservation Leaflet No 5* gives the names of wood preservative specialists and services available throughout the country.

Woodworm

The presence of woodworm in property often comes to light only at the time of a change of ownership, usually as a result of the purchaser's survey. People notice woodworm in their furniture, but in structural timbers it can go unseen for many years, because it is either hidden beneath floor-coverings or in shut-away places, such as the roof-space or cupboards under the stairs.

'Worm' is really a misnomer; the enemy is a form of beetle, but it is in its grub, or 'caterpillar', stage that we are most aware of it. This is the period during its life-cycle when it bores its way through houses and furniture. Generally, the presence of flight holes (usually circular) is the first sign of woodworm infestation. The hole is made by the pupa when it has reached its adult stage and bites its way out into the open air. The hole is not, as some people think, made by the beetle itself to deposit its eggs.

In England, there are several types of beetle which infest houses in this way. Firstly, there is the common furniture beetle, which is another misnomer as, for every single beetle infesting furniture, there must be thousands infesting structural timbers. There is considerable evidence that infestation from this particular beetle is increasing, probably the result of the vast importing of soft wood for building purposes. The result of a recent survey showed that more than 75 per cent of the buildings examined were sufficiently infested to require treatment by experts.

The common furniture beetle flies and can either come into the house from the outside or from infected timber within the house. It looks for crevices in which to lay its eggs. This is why it chooses rough, structural timbers, such as the undersides of floorboards, the undersides of drawers, the feet of chairs and tables, These are just the sort of places which are forgotten about, and it is not until the full-grown beetle emerges, after its maturation, through the french-polished surface of your favourite piece of furniture that you realize what is happening.

Death-watch beetle appeared in only 4·3 per cent of the buildings examined in the survey mentioned above. This is only likely to be found in older buildings in which the structural timber is of hardwood. Oak is the most common timber attacked although, occasionally, softwood is attacked if it is near some infested hardwood, as the attack always originates there. The death-watch beetle cannot fly; it makes its home in the deadwood of hardwood trees and infects the timber in this way.

The house longhorn beetle appears in abundance in northwest Surrey; elsewhere, its distribution seems to be sparse. The infestations occur mainly in the roof-space of the house, and this is thought to be due to the peculiar micro-climate – very hot in summer and very cold in winter. Because roof-spaces are seldom visited, house longhorn beetle infestations seldom come to light before a great deal of damage has been done.

Weevils are another localized problem. These turn up in London.

With all these varieties of beetle, it is important to go to a professional firm for advice and treatment. They all have different life cycles, appear in different sorts of woods and go for different places. In the past, woodworm has not been considered to be an acute problem, but not that the rate of infestation has increased so markedly, it is wise to take precautions. You should avoid bringing infested furniture into a house and check that there is none mouldering away in attics. Old wicker baskets are particularly vulnerable: made of willow twigs, they are the common furniture beetle's favourite place for laying its eggs, as its larvae seem to find the wood particularly enticing.

Any new work done should be carried out in timber which has been previously pressure-treated. This should be spelled out in full in the specification to your builder. Pressure treatment means that the whole body of the wood is protected, however, it is cut or worked subsequently. It will cost about 10 per cent more than using untreated wood, but the extra cost is a sound investment. Some treatments colour the timber green, others are colourless when dried out, so it is as well to go into this beforehand if you are proposing to seal rather than paint timber. Carpenters tend to dislike using timber treated in this way but I think it is because it is not ordered sufficiently early and is still tacky to handle when they have to work it. It is wise, therefore, to ensure that it is ordered in good time. Before taking on an old house, it is worth getting it surveyed by one of the nationally-known firms, such as Rentokil, who will not only discover precisely the degree and type of infestation, but will also be able to treat it in the appropriate manner, with a 20 year guarantee. This is very important as, in doing so, they will be able to ensure against re-infestation in the same area.

There are several useful leaflets on woodworm and its treatment, available from the Timber Development and Research Association. This body will also put you in touch with professional firms who carry out timber servicing of the sort I have described above.

Windows

It is of great importance to maintain the existing architectural idiom of a house, particularly when inserting any new doors or windows into the street façade. It is appalling to see a row of pleasant, or at least consistent, façades ruined by the introduction of a new window frame quite different from the rest. Sadly, planning authorities are not nearly strict enough about this.

If you want to add dormer windows, clearly these don't affect the main façade in the same way, and, at the back of the house, particularly on the ground floor, wide floor-to-ceiling sliding glazed doors might open up a sitting-room to a sunny garden and be absolutely justified. It is the street scene that one should try to preserve.

If you take on a terrace house, the windows you are most likely to find will be sash ones. If they are in such a bad state of repair that they need replacing, you have the following possibilities. Where the framing is fairly sturdy, you may be able to buy matching replacements off the peg, from a firm such as Bolton & Paul, who have a wide range of sizes which, with a little packing, can be adapted to most openings. They come both with single-paned sashes and with the sashes broken up by glazing bars into small panes, which can be useful when you are matching up with a façade of small-paned windows. However, the fine sections of many old sash windows are too expensive and difficult to produce today and, if you have to strip out crumbling windows of this kind, the best course is to replace them with aluminium sashes as the metal is able to maintain the same fine lines and small sections as the original. Aluminium windows also come in a great range of sizes and, again, with packing you should be able to suit virtually any opening. They are a good investment, as they will last indefinitely, need no maintenance and are fitted with effective, permanent draught stripping. They come ready-glazed and it is possible to buy versions which will take double-glazed panels. These will help to control heat loss, but a second frame is more effective for sound insulation (see page 185). Aluminium sash windows are available in a range of different coloured finishes apart from the pale matt grey of natural aluminium. With white window reveals, these are durable and look virtually white so that painting is hardly necessary.

Glass louvres also have advantages worth considering. It is possible, for example, to clean both sides from the inside of the house. The blades of glass can be removed should the wooden outer frame or the reveal of the window need repainting, which is a great convenience if the house is a tall one and otherwise needing long ladders. People worry that louvres can be draughty, but one firm which makes them, Beta Aluminium Products Ltd, guarantees their windows are draught- and weather-proof in the British climate. Because there is no intermediate framing, you do get maximum light through the opening. They can be made to fill almost any opening.

Dormer windows allow attics to be opened up and give added height to rooms with sloping ceilings. If you want as much light as possible to penetrate, then get your builder to glaze the sides of the dormer, as well as its face. Avoid filling up a dormer window with a lot of heavy framing as you cut out some of the possible light. Louvres are a good solution; so is a top-hung casement or an aluminium sash.

Where skylights are wanted, the only read-made one I know, which I can safely recommend, is made by Velux Ltd., of Gunnels Wood Road, Stevenage, Herts. These are double-glazed, come with their own prefabricated flashing and can have a blind fixed between the inner and outer frames. They are suitable for any roof pitch, so long as it is not less than 30 degrees. They are easy to open for ventilation and can be swung through 135 degrees so that the outside face can be cleaned easily.

For a room to be comfortably-lit, it not only requires enough light but also light of the right kind. Our eyes can respond to a very wide range of lighting conditions, but they only work within a limited part of this range at any one time. For comfort, avoid extreme contrasts of brightness and shadow, which tire the eyes, and attempt to achieve a gradual transition from the bright source of light – the window – to the more shadowed parts of the room. This is as important with daylight as it is with artificial light.

Rooms are lit by direct and indirect light. The direct light is governed by the size and shape of the windows and their position in the wall. Indirect light is reflected back from pale surfaces inside and outside the room. It is essential that windows are free from dark or shadowed areas around them, a circumstance that will cause glare when seen against the sky, and it follows that window reveals and heads should be white or very light in colour, both inside and out; so should the frame and the glazing bars on the inside. For this reason, window openings should be unobstructed. The thick walls of old houses usually have splayed reveals or richly-moulded architraves which, as long as they are not covered with dark curtains and heavy pelmets, control glare naturally. Where possible, curtains should be hung outside reveals to allow as much light as possible to enter and where you wish to avoid the direct glare of bright sunlight, you can modulate it by using awnings, venetian blinds or fixed louvres.

Windows on one wall create rather flat lighting effects to a room and, as the window-wall itself receives no direct light, the contrast between window and wall can produce glare. Both these effects can be offset by inserting a window in another wall as well. Even a tiny window will give the space in the room a more plastic quality. Where this is not practical, something similar can be achieved by glazing the door or a panel over it so that light comes through from another source, or by using large mirrors to rebound the light from a different angle.

Doors

If one type of front door is common to your terrace, it is worth trying to match it up with this, even if it means replacing your existing door. Formal houses need the richness of a panelled front door, and the orderly and symmetrical placing of door furniture.

Once inside the house, however, it depends upon what you find. If there are panelled doors and you only need to add one or two new ones, I think it is worth trying to match up again with the existing design. Bolton & Paul, Magnet and specialist firms, such as The Door Store, have some traditional-type panelled doors which may be similar to the one you want to match. You may be able to use unwanted doors from other parts of the house, or your builder may be demolishing a building of a similar age and be able to rescue some.

If the existing inside doors are battered, or even missing, then you could replace them with a panelled version appropriate to the house, or use a modern flush door. The problem of using a modern flush door where you have fairly richly-moulded architraves and other decorative details is how you treat the door. If you simply paint it to match the rest of the woodwork, it tends to look flat and 'blind', and it can be more effective to use one with a veneered face so that the colour and figuring of the wood provides some richness of its own in contrast to the surrounding wall. Doors with glass panels above and below the central locking bar can be extremely useful in opening up vistas and letting light through the house. They also marry in happily with most panelled doors, and are often useful as a means of borrowing light for staircases and landings which otherwise would have to be lit artificially. They do, of course, pose the problem of privacy in some rooms. Where you want to use glass in this way, but need screening at the same time, obscured glass will help, but it is important to use a traditional one and not one of the brash modern patterns. There is a very fine ribbed version, for example, which is very like the sort of glass one finds in old houses. If you want to see an extensive range of glass designs, the Building Centre always has an exhibition, and either James Clarke & Eaton or Pilkingtons will send you leaflets of those they make.

Stable-type doors needn't be limited to the country. They can be very pleasant to have where a kitchen opens into a garden as it allows you to let in sun and air at the top half, while keeping children and pets safely in or out, as the case may be. Cat flaps are particularly worth having in towns. Vets always say that cats shouldn't be left out at night as this is when they get infected with diseases and it is the most likely time for the cat-snatchers to operate. With a cat flap, you can leave a cat happily by itself in the day, but give it the chance of a quick escape from its enemies.

Door furniture

Door and cupboard handles, coat hooks and other decorative ironmongery are all important accessories which should be chosen carefully to be consistent with the scale and character of the house. If you propose to gut the house completely, and to re-design the interior in a contemporary idiom, there are wide ranges of good-looking modern door furniture to choose from – many of them architect-designed – and for these you can get advice from your nearest Building Centre or from the Design Centre in the Haymarket. Where you are maintaining the existing character of the house, traditional patterns are still produced by many manufacturers. Beardmore, 4 Percy Street, London, W1, is probably the best place in the country for traditional ironmongery of every kind, but Knobs and Knockers of 65 Judd Street, London WC1, also have a good traditional range, as well as an amusing stock of good modern pop designs and Art Nouveau door furniture.

The lock most commonly used for the inside doors of houses is the 'dead' lock, where the bolt is shot by turning a key. A dead lock can be housed in the thickness of the door, when it is called a mortice lock, or fixed to the surface of the door – a rim lock. The latter type is seldom used these days, but handsome brass ones are still made which can be very useful when a door is insufficiently thick or of unsuitable material to take a mortice lock. A word or warning: when buying handles, remember that not all are suitable for rim locks, so do check that you are getting the right kind.

The modern lever handle originates from early Bauhaus designs, although there are older examples, mostly Victorian, in bronze and brass. They cost about 20 per cent more than knob handles of the same quality, but they are much easier to use. Because of the easy grip they are particularly good in places where hands are likely to be wet, where there are small children or people whose hands are incapacitated in some way.

Lever handles look particularly well on the simple face of flush doors, with the added advantage that, with narrow frames, they can be set very near the edge of the door yet still be in a comfortable position for the hand, with no danger of bruised knuckles.

The gripping part of a lever handle should be at least three inches long – if anything slightly more – but for a satisfactory spring action, the end should not be more than 4 inches from the centre of the shank. Some people prefer a lever handle with the end curled in towards the door as it is less likely to catch sleeves and pockets. Designs with sharp edges should be avoided. In fact, it is always better to judge lever handles by their feel rather than their looks. Those with the broad, rather than narrow, edge uppermost, seem the most comfortable to grip.

The rose is the round disc between the handle and the door. These are not purely decorative; they are there to provide a good bearing for the handle – particularly necessary with lever handles. However, many lever handles are now set on a base plate which incorporates the keyhole. This gives a more secure bearing for the handle than a rose, especially in thin doors, since the screws of the plate can be well clear of the lock.

A lever handle should never be fitted on one side of a door and a knob handle on the other. The stronger springing necessary for the action of the lever handle makes it difficult to operate the knob, while if the springing allows the knob to move easily, the lever handle will sag in time.

Knob handles are made in a great variety of materials – wood, iron, aluminium and plain china designs are the least expensive, but should not be disregarded on this account. Round black or white china ones look handsome set on painted or natural wood-panelled doors. With a narrow gold panel added to their face, they are a good alternative to solid brass in a more sophisticated house. Painted china, brass, satin-finished chromium plate, bronze, perspex and glass are all more expensive. Perspex is largely replacing glass for handles as it is practically indistinguishable from glass in appearance (although not so cold to touch), and costs considerably less.

Drop handles have a more limited use than other kinds as they are not so easy to manipulate, but they are useful when it is necessary to avoid any projection of the door handle, such as when two doors open against each other at right-angles.

Finger plates are tending to go out of fashion for domestic use. Originally, they evolved from the need to protect the flat paint used on woodwork in earlier times, which could not be washed as easily as the gloss and eggshell finishes we have today. Moreover, the polyurethane seals with which wood is now finished do not show finger marks in the same way as traditional French polish does. However, finger plates do look good on the larger, more splendidly panelled doors and are still available in many different materials to match modern as well as antique door handles. Escutcheon plates, again, are not essential, but unless a rim lock or some sort of base plate carries the handle and incorporates the keyhole, they do give a neat finish to the keyhole opening and are frequently sold as a set with the door handles.

Rising butt hinges have three considerable advantages over the usual kind and are well worth fitting. They have a self-closing action and lift the door as it opens so that it can clear a pile carpet yet still be reasonably draught-proof when shut. The full rise is about a $\frac{1}{2}$-inch. They also allow you to lift the door off the frame without unscrewing the hinges.

Existing brass door furniture can be lacquered with a clear Shellac after it has been cleaned with metal polish. This should make cleaning unnecessary for several months, although obviously the amount of wear the door has will determine the length of time the lacquer will last.

New brass door furniture comes already lacquered and should not be touched with metal polish. Nor should you use metal polish or emery-paper on any other metal door furniture. Manufacturers advise that all other kinds should be washed with soap and water, then polished with a soft cloth. However, treatment with furniture polish does improve the appearance of wood, aluminium, chromium plate and bronze handles.

Burglar-proofing

A great deal can be done to outwit the burglar and, with increase in crime, it is essential to make secure all the vulnerable places in your house. In many cases, insurance companies insist on it anyway, although it is not necessarily the monetary value of what is stolen that is the greatest worry. The resulting mess – drawers tipped onto the floor, their contents trampled underfoot, locked writing- and jewel-cases broken open and so on – is often more upsetting.

If you fit adequate locks and appropriate safeguarding devices – and use them – this will discourage all but the most professional burglars, and it is not likely that they will bother you unless they are certain that you keep valuable jewels, furs, pictures or other such objects in the house. But any old bolt or lock won't do. The cheaper ones are easy to fiddle and force, and you can be sure that even an amateur burglar will know how to do this.

There are two ways of fitting up your house. You can either go to specialist firms, such as Banham and Chubb, who will both advise you on the most suitable locks and bolts for every opening and install them for you (this can cost as little as £50 for the whole house) or you can check every window and door of the house yourself and get a good local locksmith to provide the appropriate fittings to secure them.

Don't rely on an ordinary cylinder lock for the front door, as it is easily forced. If you already have one, then add a five lever deadlock (the minimum British Standard number of levers), or, alternatively, fit a new lock of the kind that Ingersoll make, which is a combined cylinder and deadlock. This can be locked both from the inside and outside making the lever inoperable from both sides, so that even if a burglar succeeds in getting his hand through the letter box or breaking a glass panel in the door he still will not be able to get in.

There is a lot to be said for fixing a door chain, as it does enable you to see and talk to whoever is outside without the person being able to force an entry. This can be reassuring if you are in the house by yourself at night. Again, this will be useless unless it is a really sturdy one, such as Chubb makes, which cannot be broken by a sharp thrust. A spy lens, which is a tiny magnifying glass set at eye level in the middle of the door, enables you to see anybody outside the door even if they are crouching immediately in front of it. A light outside the front door makes the spy lens equally useful at night, and certainly discourages any unauthorized person from tampering with the locks when it is dark.

Doors into the garden, French doors, and kitchen doors should have locks with at least five levers. These are difficult to open with a skeleton key. A version is made which cannot even be sawn through, as the locking bolt simply spins around under the saw. If your lock isn't of such a sophisticated variety, then a sturdy bolt top and bottom will resist forcing, even if the lock is broken.

Best of all for french doors are the espanolet bolts that are common on the Continent which make it impossible to force the door.

You can restrict a burglar's movements even if he has managed to force an entry into one of the rooms by locking all room doors from the hall and landing side at night.

On the whole, burglars avoid breaking glass to get in. They may make a small hole to get at a lock or a catch, but they are generally reluctant to climb through broken glass. Double glazing apparently provides a very good deterrent.

Sash windows often have catches which are extremely easy to lever open with a penknife, and should be replaced by a 'fitch' or a similar catch which cannot be forced open in the same way. Or you can fit 'Acorn' stops which are equally suitable, as these will let you open both top and bottom sashes enough for ventilation, or for the cat to get in and out but too little for anyone to squeeze their way in. Locking 'stops' work in the same way, but give greater protection, as it would still be impossible to move the sash without using the lock's proper key, even if the glass is broken near the stops. Casement and pivot windows can now have stay fittings which prevent entry even when left partly open, and it is possible to fit locking bolts and locking window catches which will completely secure the window when it is closed.

Windows opening directly on to pavements or basement areas would be worth fitting with a grille. Skylights and trapdoors to the roof are a popular way in for burglars: they get inside any empty house and work their way across the rooftops. If the trapdoor is a solid one then it is enough to bolt it securely from the inside. If it is a glass skylight it helps to fit it with wired glass (Georgian wired polished plate looks perfectly acceptable), and to fix a locking bolt.

Fireplaces

So long as you want to maintain the traditional character of your house, don't rush to rip out any good-looking fireplace without giving yourself time for second thoughts. If your house is a small one, or a large one that you are dividing into self-contained flats, you might well be able to exploit the sitting-room fireplace and use the opening to house a back boiler system which can run your central heating and so save boiler space elsewhere.

Even if you don't use your sitting-room fireplace for a central heating unit, it is generally worth hanging on to it unless you are changing the character of the room completely. The flue does provide natural ventilation which can be useful where windows are double-glazed and draught-stripped. Fires can be very welcome on chilly grey summer evenings when the central heating is turned off, and they can provide a second line of defence in the event of a power cut. If you don't want to be bothered with coal, you could fit a gas or electric radiant/convector into the opening.

Handsomely-proportioned surrounds are often disguised by toffee-coloured varnish or dark green paint. If you find wood beneath, and the room is a large one, it could look well simply left in its stripped condition. If the room is a small one, the surround will probably look best painted or tiled to match the rest of the woodwork. You might even be able to find enough attractive old ones in a junk yard or lying forgotten in a corner in a tiler's warehouse. Or, instead of re-tiling, you could infill the frame with panels of slate or beaten metal; or you could use narrow ribbed asbestos, painted matt black, which has the crisp attractive appearance of ribbed cast-iron, a favourite Georgian and Regency material for

fireplaces. Alternatively, you could leave the outer frame and open up the recess, lining it with any of the materials just mentioned and setting a free-standing fire in the opening. Free-standing fires and enclosed stoves are particularly efficient and are available in both traditional and more contemporary models. Allied Iron Founders and Heaton both make good-looking traditional ones. The Acorn and the Pither are handsome modern versions.

Where you want to retain the traditional character of your house and the previous owners have ripped out the original fireplaces and replaced them with porridge-coloured horrors, you need to find a suitable replacement for the sitting-room. Too many people try to solve the problem with the over-refined, undersize, carved pine type or, even worse, the mock Adam versions. Be sure you find one that is really in scale and in period with the room. If you are using an architect, he should be able to design one for you or know where to find one that suits. Some firms specialize in these. London's St Pancras Borough Council is particularly enterprising in that it carefully rescues all the good features such as iron railings, fan-lights, fireplaces, etc, from demolished houses, so that they are available for people converting and restoring property in the borough.

It is worth remembering that, apart from providing a traditional place for the clock, invitations and family photographs, a mantelshelf has a practical purpose: it serves to deflect the warm air rising from the fire into the centre of the room. This not only yields a more comfortably heated room, but it also prevents the air from rising straight up to leave dust marks on the chimney-breast.

191

Slate and marble wash-stand tops will often provide handsome hearths. I have seen the moulded back and sides of a marble washstand effectively used to make a handsome cantilevered mantelshelf. Its strong simple mouldings were absolutely right for the room.

When you are carrying out the major conversion of a warehouse, for example, or you are going to gut a room completely, but want to retain the fire, a raised hearth can turn the inevitable and necessary projection of the hearth into a virtue. A raised hearth has several advantages. It enables you to install under-hearth ventilation without disturbing the floor, and provides a useful long, low fireside table or bench which becomes an integral feature of the room, even in summertime, when a fireplace can look sad and neglected. You can, of course, more simply raise the position of the fire itself to 9 inches or a foot above the floor and insert one of the 'hole in the wall fireplaces' where the metal frame is set directly into the brickwork with the plaster running right up to it. If your room is very narrow, however, a raised hearth could make it appear even more so.

If you decide to get rid of a fireplace, it is important that the room should be redesigned in such a way that it does not look as if something is missing. You must provide a strong alternative focal element. In bedrooms for instance, you could develop the chimney-breast as the bedhead wall, or by utilizing the depth of the side recesses, run a cupboard front across the entire wall with the shallower central section fitted with shelves and drawers. In the dining-room, it could be the place to put a wide sideboard, in the study a substantial desk. Where rooms are very narrow, you can seem to double their width by facing the chimney-breast wall, floor-to-ceiling and side-to-side, with looking glass. In a children's room, you could face the lower half with blackboard and the upper half with pin-up board. In the sitting-room, where the chimney-breast is wide enough, it could be the place to put a sofa, so that the focus of the room is turned inwards towards the centre, rather than facing towards one wall. Where the fireplace is being removed and there are no recesses on either side, the wall can still retain its focal pull if you line it floor-to-ceiling with irregularly-spaced shelves to take books, hi-fi equipment, a handsome clock, some plants, a mirror and so on.

The alternative to blocking off the fireplace is to open up the chimney-breast into a large central recess, which can house shelves, a cupboard or a piece of furniture. In a kitchen, it could accommodate the bulky depth of a refrigerator or a built-in oven so that their faces run flush with a bank of shallow cupboards on either side. Or, if you are having a separate hob unit, you could build this into the recess, fitting the flue-opening above with an extractor fan. In a guest bedroom or dressing-room, the recess could house a basin set in a counter top and so double as a dressing-table.

Storage

Built-in storage has many valuable advantages. Banks of cupboards set against walls between bedrooms and along party walls considerably improve sound insulation, or, built along outside walls, give added heat insulation. Storage can also exploit any recesses in a house, such as those commonly found at the side of chimney-breasts, or fill in the awkward corner formed by the sloping roofs of attics. It can be valuable in children's rooms, running at bench-height along walls and under windows to provide seating (softened, if you like, with slab cushions) or low table tops for games of every kind. It can help reshape awkward spaces – as when you run a bank of cupboards across the narrow end of a long thin room.

Built-in storage makes a lot of the more traditional types of furniture – wardrobes, sideboards, chests of drawers and so on – unnecessary. Unless you already have a lot of furniture, there is everything to be said for limiting what you buy to tables, seating, odd chairs, sofas and, of course, beds, and then either build the rest in or buy unit storage furniture, which serves the same purpose. Grouping and organizing storage in this way can make small rooms seem far less cluttered, free circulation and make cleaning considerably easier. The useful anonymity of built-in and unit storage furniture also allows rooms to serve satisfactorily two of more different functions. Because of the high premium put on space these days, this is becoming an increasingly important consideration when furnishing any room. Dining-rooms can double as children's play-rooms or studies; guest rooms as sewing-rooms – there are many permutations. No two families will want the same facilities; no two houses will offer the same possibilities. What really matters is to stop limiting rooms to their traditional purposes and look at them afresh, simply as spaces to be lived in.

If possible, you should combine built-in storage with any structural changes you are making. The time to think about all the storage space you are likely to need over the next ten years or so is while you still have the builders in the house and extra cupboards can be incorporated into new work. It is worth allowing for far more storage space than you feel you could ever need. With bulk-buying becoming increasingly popular, generous storage becomes more essential. Hobbies and sports make considerable demands on storage space; so does any kind of do-it-yourself activity. Then there are all the things that are used only once a year, such as Christmas decorations and annual holiday luggage.

The way you treat built-in storage will depend on the character of the room. But, whatever the character, it is important to maintain the room's architectural consistency.

MAINS SERVICES

Services – plumbing, heating, electricity and so on – should be the servants, not the masters, of the house. Somtimes an existing flue may suggest the position of a boiler, or a run of drains makes it easier to plan your bathrooms and kitchen on one side of the house rather than the other, but don't let such considerations interfere with you own overall plan. Modern equipment and installation techniques can fit heating, plumbing and wiring almost anywhere in the house so long as you allow for them from the outset.

Water, gas and electricity are all operated by regional area boards and, although there are some national regulations, practices and prices do vary, if only slightly, from district to district. The local authority will advise you over any problems connected with drainage. You can also take any queries on water supply to them and they will refer you to the local area water board if the problem is beyond them. If the house has no gas supply and you want to use gas, you simply contact the local gas board. Similarly the local electricity board will advise you on their tariffs, installation and equipment.

Mains drainage

If the building you are converting is not on the mains, but the main sewer is by the road, your builder can arrange with the local authority to make a connexion. The local authority will make a charge for this and the builder charges for excavation and pipe-laying.

At every branch of the drain and every change of direction there has to be an unobstructed lidded man-hole to provide access for rodding in case the drain-pipes get blocked. Where the area is to be paved, ensure that the man-hole lies parallel with the lines of the paving to match the overall pattern.

In most older properties, waste from the bath, basin and sink will be carried to the outside of the house and discharged over an open-headed pipe or gulley, while the soil or lavatory waste is taken quite separately underground to the drains. Where existing plumbing has to be replaced building regulations now allow both waste and soil to be connected directly to a single soil vent pipe which can be situated inside the house. This not only avoids a tangle of ugly piping on the outside of the house but the danger of freezing in wintertime. Soil vent pipes and internal drain connexions now can be carried out in tough plastic piping which takes up less room and is capable of tighter turns than the old salt-glazed or iron kinds. Try to plan so that all piping, whether drainage, water supply or central heating, is concealed in the structure of the building – in the thickness of the floors, inside cupboards and ducts, etc. In towns and cities, both household waste and rainwater are taken to the main sewer. Where you find you have to replace gutters and downpipes, plastic and glass fibre ones make good sense, especially on tall buildings, as they never rust, crack or need painting, and are easy to fit.

Mains water

If you need to connect mains water to the property, you will have to pay for all the cost of the connexion from the mains. However, this is an item which, along with any other connexion to mains services, would be covered by an improvement grant. If your house is a large one and you are considering converting some of it into self-contained units, each unit will have to have its own independent water supply direct from the mains. Where a new connexion has to be made, the water board makes a 'T'-joint at a point on the mains nearest you property, for which they charge about five pounds. The excavation work necessary to make this connexion will have to be done by your builder, who also lays the service pipe which leads to the house from it. This supply pipe is your responsibility. There has to be a stop-cock at the point where the supply enters the house, to cut off the mains supply when necessary. It is important to know where this is so that it can be turned off when you go on holiday or there is some repair work to be done. Your local authority will probably demand that you have additional stop-cocks to control the supply to the kitchen sink, the hot water storage tank and any lavatory cisterns.

One pipe from the mains supply will feed the cold tap at the kitchen sink; another will rise up to feed the cold water storage tank. This means that, if you want to soften the water, the softener can be connected to the feed to the cold water tank only, leaving you with hard water for drinking and cooking if you prefer it (see section on water softening). The local water board will lay down the requirement on size of a cold water storage tank. Where it is necessary to fit a new one, glass fibre is the best choice as it is very light, tough and non-corrosive, as well as being self-insulating. These storage tanks can be supplied with lids; these are worth while having as they do keep out dust, insects and the occasional rat. When the position of your storage tank is being planned,

don't forget that, if you want a shower using water from the hot water system, the base of the tank should be at least 3 feet above the shower head, in order to get sufficient pressure. If this is not possible, the shower can be supplied from an independent water heater taken directly from the mains (see section on water heating).

See that your builder fits Garston-type valves, developed by the Building Research Station, as these are the most efficient. A silencer, which is a plastic pipe running from the valve down below water level, is also worth having, as the incoming water entering the tank below, rather than above, water level makes far less noise. Feed pipes from the cold water tank run to the hot water storage tank, the lavatory cisterns and the cold taps of baths and basins. The lavatory cistern, too, should be fitted with a Garston valve and silencer. If you want drinking water from any of the cold taps, you should specify this so that a pipe direct from the mains can be taken to feed the tap in question.

Domestic hot water

Hot water can be provided in two quite different ways. It can either be heated comparatively slowly and stored until it is wanted in large or small insulated storage cylinders, or it can be heated at the moment of use from fittings which supply one or more hot taps.

If you decide to use a boiler to provide central heating, it could probably provide you domestic hot water as well, but you should check with your heating engineer or contractor whether it is economic to keep the boiler going all through the summer months simply for hot water. Boilers vary considerably in their ability to keep up the same efficiency at the lower outputs involved, when they are producing only domestic hot water. If they are not capable of fairly high efficiencies on smaller loads, then it may well be more economic to turn them off completely for the summer and use an electric immersion heater.

With back boiler central heating run on solid fuel, it is always wise to provide an immersion heater to take over in the summer when you won't want a fire. In some cases it may make better sense, if you want to ensure that you get as much heat as possible out of your radiators, to limit your back boiler to central heating only and to heat your water entirely by some other means.

Warm air heating systems frequently do not provide for domestic hot water, which requires that separate water heating equipment is installed. When this is necessary, it is generally most economic to continue to use the fuel used for the central heating, if it is either electricity or gas, as you will get a better tariff rate. Independent gas water boilers for domestic hot water are available with either conventional or balanced flues, and electric storage water heaters are available in a great range of sizes. The latter are so well insulated that, they leak almost no heat at all. Certainly, if you are heating a house by any night storage method, it is worth

heating the water, too, at the same cheap rate (see notes on the White Meter, page 196).

The storage method of water heating tends to be cheaper to run, whatever the fuel, if you are likely to use a lot of hot water. However, when two baths have been drawn you may have to wait for half- to three-quarters-of-an-hour before another can be taken. One way of improving this situation is to have pump acceleration of the hot water primary circuit of your hot water tank, which speeds up the recovery rate considerably. (The gas board incorporates this in all its Guaranteed Warmth schemes.) A 30-gallon hot water tank would then be sufficient for a small household with only one bathroom: for anything larger, find room for a 50-gallon tank.

Instantaneous water heaters are now available run on gas or electricity. They can supply continuous hot water at any time of the day and night and will be more economical if the use of hot water is limited. Instantaneous water heaters are worth considering if you are converting some of your house into small flats. The gas versions can be multi-point, which means that more than one tap can be supplied by the same heater. They do, however, have the disadvantage that while one hot tap is running the pressure of the other hot taps will be reduced. Electric instantaneous water heaters are a fairly new development and, as I write, only small versions are available, for one tap only. They are large enough to supply continuous hot water to an individual sink or basin, and could be useful for an independent bed-sitting-room or flatlet, or in a large house, where hot water pipes would otherwise have to go a long distance to supply a tap in an outlying sink. They are also useful where a shower is wanted too high up in the house for a proper head of water from the storage tank to be available. Another way of getting over the problem of outlying sanitary fittings, at the same

194

time avoiding the wastage of hot water left unused in long lengths of pipe, is to pump-circulate the domestic hot-water supply.

It is good sense not to set the thermostat which governs the temperature of the water at too high a temperature. Between 120°F and 140°F is safest. Set at this temperature, there is not danger of small children scalding themselves and in a hard water district where immersion heaters are used, it minimizes the likelihood of scale building up on the heating element and so shortening its life. It goes without saying that if you have a hot water storage system which does not come in its own insulated container, it pays to insulate your hot water tank as well as you possibly can. The standard jackets sold by builders' merchants are just not enough. Let the builder fix a rigid casing of hardboard or plywood around the tank and fill the space between this casing and the tank with kapok. Sawdust and mineral wool are not really suitable for such a position as they are so unpleasant to handle should some repair work have to be done on the tank or piping.

Water softening

Although rain water is 'soft', tap water is all too frequently 'hard'. Percolating through various earth layers before reaching you, most tap water collects, *en route*, too many chemicals – in the form of calcium and magnesium salts – for our comfort. A certain amount of these salts is precipitated when water is boiled – hence the deposit left on the inside of kettles and pipes. This is called 'temporary' hardness. Other salts, unaffected by boiling, need chemical treatment to remove them, and it is for this 'permanent' hardness that water-softening processes come in.

The savage effects of hard water are overlooked by most people because damage develops slowly. Yet once done, it can be extremely expensive to put right. The most serious damage is likely to be the pipes and tank of your hot water system. With furred-up pipes you may well need to use a third more fuel than you should, as well as letting yourself in for the expense of having pipes and boiler chemically de-scaled. Where hard water also does great harm is in such equipment as washing-machines, washing-up machines and water heaters. Pipes and heating elements get furred up and motors wear out more quickly, so that their operation is not only less efficient, but maintenance and replacement are more frequent.

With hard water, not only will you use twice as much soap and detergent as you need, but the hardness creates a scum which matts woollens and takes the lustre out of fabrics. Hard water is harmful to hair and skin. Soft water is kind and makes shaving much easier. Plates drip dry without a smear and glasses sparkle as never before.

Your local Water Board will tell you how hard the water is in your area and whether you should take special precautions. Hardness is measured in degrees, anything over 14°C (Clark's scale) being considered hard. London water, for instance, is about 18°C. You can test for yourself whether the water in your area is hard by noting how much soap you need to make a measured amount of tap water lather. In London, it take 2 ounces of soap to neutralize the hardness of a bucket of tap water before a lather is produced.

Although hard water is usually associated with the presence of lime and calcium, iron salts in the water also produce scaling. They stain the water brown and often occur when the water is apparently soft in every other way. So, however silky water feels, and however good a lather you have, it is wise to check whether an iron scale is not remorselessly building up in the hot water system. If you decide to use any of the recommended installations, the manufacturers will make an analysis of your water and install a softener with appropriate chemicals.

The water-softening system you choose, of course, will depend on where you live and the size of your household. There are some simple precautions to be taken. If you use a boiler to heat your water, check there is an indirect hot-water cistern, where the water actually used is heated indirectly by a closed circuit of water which comes in direct contact with the boiler. This is essential in hard-water districts. If you use an electric immersion heater or a gas instantaneous heater, have the fitter see that the water temperature is not set too high – just above 120°F is sensible. The hotter water gets, the more chalk it precipitates.

If you can get at your cold water tank, there are several products which you can suspend in the water tank itself. These mostly come in canister form, their contents lasting about six months. Softflo softens the water and, it is claimed, breaks down gradually any existing build-up of scale. Micromet doesn't actually soften the water but acts to stabilize the chemicals which cause water hardness and so prevents a build-up of scale. It can also be used to control the corrosion of iron and galvanized tanks in soft water areas and will eliminate 'red' water. Neither of these products has any colour, taste or smell, and both are entirely harmless to use.

By treating the water in the cold tank in this way, pipes, hot water tank and any equipment using hot or cold water from them, benefit. However, a problem arises with some dish-washing machines which take in cold water only, as this will be drawn directly from the untreated mains supply pipe in the kitchen. To overcome this, in cases where it is not convenient to bring in a special cold water supply from the storage tank, there are small independent water-softening units that can be connected directly into a washing-up machine. The Sari by Essex Water Softeners, and the Picco by Cord Chemical Co, are two such units. Some washing-up machines, of course, such as the Westinghouse and the Miele, incorporate their own water-softening device.

All your water can be treated to prevent scaling at the

point where the mains enter the house. There are two ways of doing this, one electrical and one chemical. With either system, the de-scaling unit is small, roughly 12 inches long and 9 inches in diameter, and can be installed by a local plumber. Aquastat makes the electrical version which needs no attention. Chemical units are the Libelle, the Dulcomat and the Picco. These need recharging every six months or so.

Without question, the most satisfactory method is to soften all the water that goes into your cold water storage tank. This still leaves you the possibility of hard water from your kitchen cold tap if you prefer the taste. It is also possible to have lavatory cisterns taken out of the circuit so that softened water isn't wastefully flushed away.

The more automatic the water-softening unit, the more expensive. However, unless your household is a very large one, the modern units are compact and sufficiently unobtrusive to be slotted alongside other units in the kitchen. At the most they will require refilling with regenerating salt two or three times a year. Those requiring some manual control need recharging rather more frequently.

If you dislike the flavour chlorination gives your mains tap water – some city water tastes pretty nasty even though it is perfectly safe to drink – there is now a range of reliable equipment that can filter and purify. Young Culligan, a firm with considerable experience in water treatment in America, make a handsome unit which is plumbed permanently into the cold water supply at the kitchen sink. No electricity or chemicals are required, but the filters have to be replaced yearly. British Berkefeld Filters, Tonbridge, Kent, make a small portable filter, the Osoclear, which can be simply connected to the kitchen tap. This is filled with a special grade of activated carbon, and the Sterasyl granules which keep this fresh need renewing yearly.

The Cord Chemical Company has set up a full Water Advisory Bureau, which is not restricted to advising on its own company's products. Its staff and advisors are a consortium of water engineers, chemists, plumbers and manufacturers of products using water. The Bureau answers questions on subjects as varied as de-scaling kettles, breeding exotic fish, treating swimming-pool water, removing bath stains, curing rumbling boilers, inserting fluoride, as well as taking it out!

One of the services offered free of charge is water analysis which will often indicate the cause of a problem. Readers are advised to send a 2-ounce plastic bottle of their tap water to the Bureau for examination. The analysis is restricted to the physical characteristics of the water and not its microbiological content.

Mains gas

Your local Gas Board will bring their supply pipe to your property and provide a meter with a main cock (tap) on the mains supply side of the meter. You should know where this cock is and how to turn it off in case you suspect a leak. The meter should be easily accessible for reading, ideally from the outside of the house, so that it can be read even when nobody is at home. Where a completely new installation is necessary, get the gas board itself to carry out the work. They will charge far less than an outside firm, and you will be sure of reliable workmanship. If you are taking over an existing installation and fittings, have them tested by the gas board before you start redecorating. Both for efficiency and safety, it is worth having this done every year.

Pipe linings and burners can accumulate deposits, taps work loose and leak slightly, and water-heaters, particularly in hard water districts, need de-scaling.

Apart from gas cookers and gas pokers, all equipment using gas needs to be linked with a flue. Even where there is a flue, it is wise to have a small amount of fixed ventilation in rooms where gas equipment is used, unless it is fitted with a balanced flue. The installation of gas fittings has been revolutionized by the balanced flue, which needs nothing more than a small outlet through an outside wall. Fittings with balanced flues are particularly safe as they draw air for burning from outside, not the room itself, and are completely unaffected by changes in pressure and direction of the wind.

Mains electricity

Costs and conditions for bringing electricity to a property will vary with the different boards. Existing installations, even if fairly new, should be tested by the Electricity Board when you take on a house. Installations 30 years old or more are suspect, and if re-wiring has to be done, it is as well to get it over before you redecorate. Even if the wiring is in good order, the supply may not be designed to carry as much power as you want to use, and may need supplementing.

Every Electricity Board has its special cheap rate tariffs based on the supply conditions affecting its area. There is now an additional domestic tariff called the White Meter tariff. With this meter, you pay for all your electricity at two different rates: a day rate and a much cheaper night rate. Unlike the existing off-peak rates, this cheap night rate is not limited to certain types of equipment, such as storage radiators or hot water heating. Every piece of electrical equipment run during the night-rate hours will benefit from this cheaper tariff – refrigerators, deep-freezes, greenhouse heating, water heating, as well as such things as automatic washing-machines and dishwashers.

Wiring can be done either by the contract department of the Electricity Board or by an independent electrical contractor approved by the Board, and it is worth getting competitive quotations. The Electricity Board's inspectors check the finished installation and operate quite separately from the contract department, whose work is put through the same stringent tests as that of any outside firm. Electrical wiring should never be done by amateurs or odd-job men. Faulty installations can easily cause fire and serious shocks.

The ring main system with square holes for the plug pins is now standard practice for all new installations. All socket outlets are rated at 13 amps and can take any electrical equipment, except a standard cooker which will need a special cooker point. You should let your electrical installer know the type of cooker you propose to have as some of the larger ones demand a particularly heavy cable. With the new ring mains system, sockets are wired in a continuous ring around each floor of the house instead of each socket being wired back to the distributing board. This makes the installation much simpler and much cheaper than under the old system. Each plug has its own fuse and this can be related to the equipment used with it: a 13-amp fuse for a fire, a 5-amp fuse for a bedside lamp. If a fitting shorts, the trouble is isolated at this point and once the cause of the short is found and repaired, all you have to do is to fit another capsule fuse of the right capacity into the plug.

Lighting

Although there are a number of very good light fittings these days, there is still not nearly enough good lighting. It's not just a question of under-lighting – it is the sheer dullness of it. Many rooms that look charming by day lose all their character at night.

When planning the lighting for your house, you need to remember that it has three main purposes. Firstly, the purely functional one of being the right type and in the right place so that you can read, cook or make up your face in clear bright light without glare or strain. Secondly, it can make a great contribution to the safety of your house by high-lighting changes of level, providing two-way switches on stairs and lamps by every bedside so there is no stumbling about in the dark. Lastly, it needs to take a cue from the theatre and create atmosphere as well, especially when one room has to play a number of parts.

Before starting to analyze what sort of lighting you want, and where you want it, it is worth making sure you understand the character of the three main types of light (not lighting fittings) there are at your disposal. Some fittings give one type of light only, others two or more.

Direct light is produced by a shade which is opaque and so focuses light in one direction, or two if it is open at both ends. Direct light is extremely useful when one is working, as the opaque shade protects the eye from the glare of the bulb while the working surface is flooded with light. However, it is best not to use direct light on its own in this way in a work-room or study as the contrast of surface and shadows surrounding it will cause eye-strain. There should always be some form of background lighting in these rooms. It can be equally tiring for the eyes to watch television in a completely darkened room. You will find it far more comfortable if you have some diffused or indirect light close by to offset the brilliance of the screen. Extreme contrasts of light and shade do not matter so much with a directional fitting set low over a dining-room table, for example, where your gaze is not so likely to be concentrated on one spot.

Diffused light describes the soft glow produced when the source of light is screened by a translucent shade, such as the Japanese paper lanterns and milky white glass of old oil lamps. Wherever gentle but lively illumination is needed, wall, ceiling or table lamps with translucent shades are the ones to choose. The glare of fluorescent tubes, if left unshaded and visible to the eye, can be distracting, but fitted with a translucent shade they can provide diffused, shadowless light which is particularly useful in kitchens, bathrooms and work-rooms generally.

Fittings giving diffused light are useful for providing general lighting on staircases, in halls and as central ceiling lights in small rooms of any kind. In fact where there is to be just one light-fitting in a room (this is not recommended unless the room is extremely small) a fitting giving diffused light is the most successful.

With indirect light, the source of light is totally screened to deflect the light onto the surrounding walls, ceiling and floors. Indirect light is another means of providing general background illumination, and fluorescent tubes, concealed in alcoves or set behind battens or on top of bookshelves and pelmets, can be effectively used in this way. Indirect lighting of this kind emphasizes the shape and size of a room and can be used equally successfully in traditional or modern interiors. It is particularly useful in fine period rooms as it produces the quantity and quality of light needed without recourse of bogus-looking reproduction light fittings. Whether you are using indirect lighting in modern or traditional settings, it is essential to have sufficient fittings giving diffused or directional light in the body of the room; otherwise, the over-emphasis of walls and ceiling will create a dead area in the centre of the room.

Bad lighting can cause accidents. Stairs should always be brightly lit, particularly steps to the front door, winders on staircases and single steps in unexpected places. Double switches at the top and bottom of flights save tumbles, and if you are rewiring the house, light switches at door handle height not only look better but avoid groping around in the dark. Never be mean about the number of points you install. It is almost a case of working out how many you think you need and then doubling it.

HEATING AND INSULATION

Before rushing into a decision on central heating, and even before getting in touch with the various advisory organizations, do some homework youself. Many of the heating firms, including Ideal Standard and Potterton, produce extremely good booklets, and the Coal Utilization Council, the Gas Council, the British Electrical Development Association and Shell-Mex will all send you useful brochures on their most recent equipment, installation and financing. If you are in London, the Building Centre is well worth a visit, as there are sections devoted to the main fuels, where you can get advice on the different appliances and systems. Above all, don't by unduly influenced by friends. Their dissatisfaction with a certain method of heating may well have nothing to do with the method itself but with bad installation, inferior equipment or just that that particular method doesn't suit their particular house.

I would recommend going to a consultant heating engineer who is completely independent in his advice. He will design the system, provide a specification against which heating contractors can tender, select the most suitable contractor and then supervise the complete installation. The savings made would easily cover his fee. Sadly, many consultants haven't time to take on domestic work. However, if you are using an architect, ask his advice. He may well know an engineer who will help, or he may be able to design a scheme himself in conjunction with a good firm of heating contractors. Failing this, go to the National Heating Centre; they do invaluable work and their advice is objective. On learning about your type of house and family requirements, they will be able to assess what type of fuel and system is most appropriate; if you cannot call personally, they will send you an analysis form.

The National Heating Centre's exhibition is open to the public, free of charge, for inspection of equipment and the distribution of manufacturers' leaflets. They make a small charge for advice on a time basis. The Centre has compiled a register of reliable contractors and any work carried out by these firms is covered by a two-year protection certificate issued to the householder by the Heating Centre and backed by the British Insurance Association. Whether you go to the Heating Centre or not, you should insist that the specification for your heating system and estimate is based on the requirements of the *Guide to Good Practice for Small Bore and Warm Air* published jointly by the Heating and Ventilating Contractors' Association and the Institution of Heating and Ventilating Engineers. The National Heating Centre has no branches at present, although many towns do in fact have 'heating centres' but these are all trading organizations.

Heating comfort

While you are at the stage of considering which system will suit you best, assuming that you will insulate as well as possible you should aim at achieving the following:

1. *Warm feet and a cool head* – floor heating, skirting radiators and convectors, warm air grilles set at floor level.
2. *Heat spread evenly round the room* – skirting radiators and convectors, heated floors, heated ceilings.
3. *A heated structure* – warm floors, warm ceilings and large wall panels of low temperature heat – as this gives no loss of body heat. Continuous heating, even at low temperature, with night storage radiators, skirting or standard radiators, plus really effective insulation, can provide the same measure of comfort as the structure remains charged with heat.
4. *A source of high temperature/radiant heat* – open fires, closed stoves and radiant electric, gas and oil heaters – which is valuable, particularly for older people and young children as it is needed to counteract quickly the effect of serious chilling in cold weather.
5. *A combination of radiant and convected heat* – skirting or standard radiators, night storage radiators, heated floors,

ceiling and walls, or warm air systems, plus a source of high temperature heat. Systems or heaters which provide warm air only have to give a higher air temperature than radiator systems for the same comfort, unless they are adequately humidified.

6. *Effective ventilation* – the air in occupied rooms should be completely changed from one to one-and-a-half times per hour. In the best warm air systems, the air is humidified, filtered and recharged with fresh air from outside, as well as being warmed. With other systems, especially when a house has been efficiently draught-stripped, specific ventilation may be necessary. Flued fires or heaters can help, so do extractor fans in bathrooms and kitchens. For other rooms, Greenwood Airvac make strip adjustable ventilators that can be set inconspicuously at the top of windows. Where dryness needs offsetting, there are water troughs that can be fitted on radiators and various electrically-powered humidifiers.

Heating systems

The choice of fuel for a central heating system is always a problem, as each has advantages and disadvantages. It is sometimes argued that, in a small house, one can afford to use the more expensive fuels – gas and electricity – and keep down running costs with efficient controls and a high degree of insulation. Gas and electricity are undoubtedly the most trouble-free fuels, as well as taking up the least space. It is in the larger houses of 2,000 square feet upwards, or with more than three floors, that the real savings are shown by using oil and solid fuels.

An oil tank can be sited in a basement, but the installation has to meet some fairly stringent regulations and will inevitably cost quite a bit to carry out. If it has to be in the garden, remember that tanks now come in all shapes and sizes to fit in the space available and can be screened on top as well as around the sides with trellis and climbers.

In small town houses space will be at a premium, so the most practical heating systems to use are those which can either exploit an existing flue, such as back boiler units, work off a balanced flue which needs only an outside wall, or need no flue at all. Back boiler systems are now available fired by gas, solid fuel or oil, to run radiator systems. Their greatest advantage is that they also provide radiant heat from the main living-room fireplace, and as most town houses have one, this is a way of putting it to positive use and justifying it as a focal point. For a self-contained flat, a small house or one in which background heat only is wanted in the rest of the house, similar back boiler units are available which provide this through the circulation of warm air by fan-assisted natural convection (no ducts).

Many of the back boiler units, both radiator and warm air type, are able to provide domestic hot water as well and, apart from those fired by solid fuel, they can continue to do so independently of space heating when this isn't wanted in warm weather. With a solid fuel back boiler/radiator system, an electric immersion heater can take over from domestic hot water in the summer.

Another space-saving solution for small and medium-sized houses is the new type of compact gas-fired boiler which can be hung high on an outside wall anywhere in the house (even up in the loft) as they work off a balanced flue. A further means of taking the boiler out of the kitchen is offered by the gas-fired Servowarm system which has its tiny, but highly effective, boiler in the master radiator, which only needs to be placed against an outside wall to provide an outlet for its balanced flue.

If you are using one of the bigger gas or oil fired boilers, it may be an advantage to use one of the existing flues in the house. Certainly, where a balanced flue is not suitable, I feel this is preferable to building up a clumsy prefabricated one on the outside of the house. This need not mean taking up valuable space on the ground floor. Even though I have no fireplace opening in the basement of my own house, I found it possible to have the boiler there and run its pipe up through the back of the hearth of one of the ground-floor fireplaces, simply blocking it off from the room. When this is done, it is essential that the flue is correctly lined and the least disruptive ways of doing this is to use a system such as Rentokil's, which feeds an inflatable tube up the flue to act as a shuttering for the insulating cement which is poured down the chimney around it.

There is now a boiler for small to medium-sized houses that doesn't need a flue at all. This is the new electric Centralec system which, using the White Meter, heats the boiler by cheap-rate electricity at night and only tops up on the standard rate during the day. This electric boiler will run a small bore or microbore radiator system just like a boiler fired by any other fuel and can be placed anywhere in the house. Its sophisticated controls allow it to perform effectively at very low running costs.

Electric ceiling heating is remarkably inexpensive to install. It works best in large rooms. although the height isn't important so long as it is 7 feet 6 inches, or over, so, when ceilings in larger town houses have to be re-plastered is the time to consider ceiling heating. It is one of the most trouble-free of all heating systems and is responsive to controls, leaving the walls and floors of the room completely free for furniture and decoration.

Floor heating systems are generally not recommended in town houses as heat tends to leak into neighbouring buildings, although if you want a hard floor, such as quarry tiles in the basement, which could otherwise be cold, you might consider it there to supplement the main heating.

In small to medium houses the deep recesses often found on either side of the chimney-breast can provide useful housing for the bulkiness of night storage radiators. Shelved over, they can form a base section of a cupboard or shelving unit. Night storage radiators can now form in themselves a full central heating system. In their newest version, they are considerably more flexible – so far as control of heat output is concerned – than the old type. They give out heat for 24 hours with an automatic thermostatically-controlled boost during the afternoon and evening.

Unless the place is being extensively remade, existing terraced houses lend themselves more readily to radiator than warm air systems, but fan-assisted radiators can be extremely useful where space is short in halls and landings. Fan-assisted radiators have the advantage that they can provide a sudden quick boost of heat to warm up a house. if you have been out all day, and, in summer, they can be used as an air circulator.

In terraced houses, it is important not to destroy the formal quality of the rooms by badly-placed radiators. If you can exploit any of the existing architectural features, so much the better. If the windows are recessed, you can fit the radiator in the panel below an extended sill and, instead of hanging curtains over the entire window, have a matching blind, leaving the curtains undrawn at the sides. The recesses on either side of the chimney-breasts can take low, wide hospital radiators beneath shelving units, etc. Where these recesses are already filled with cupboards, and no fire is needed in the room, the fireplace can be ripped out and finned tubes set in the recess screened by a simple panel with space above and below for air circulation.

The alternative to the block type of radiator is to run skirting or baseboard radiators along the entire length of the outside walls, hanging curtains so that they stop just short of the radiator capping. The radiant heat and convected warm air will be directed into the room at floor level (the best for comfort) and curtains will not be damaged in any way. Panel radiators are best saved for the positions where they can be related to some design feature of the room – directly below a window sill, for example, or under a serving-hatch.

In terraced houses, with the warmth rising upwards, it is most important that an efficient system of controls is used, and it will be rewarding to have each floor controlled as a separate circuit. This will allow you to keep the bedroom floors operating at a different temperature from that of the main living-floor, thus preventing an unnecessary build-up of heat in the upper floors when they are not being used.

Air conditioning and warm air heating

Clearly, it is the people living in the centre of cities who are most in need of a fully air-conditioned environment. The sort of full air conditioning that one finds in commercial premises is still an extremely expensive installation, but many of the advantages it offers are now available within domestic warm-air systems. With any ducted warm-air system, for example, it is possible to fit a humidifier. Honeywell make a control which ensures that the moisture added is appropriate exactly to the required humidity and this, used in conjunction with their air cleaner, provides air that is virtually free of dust and pollen. Such a combination can give tremendous relief to anyone suffering from asthma or any other respiratory complaint, quite apart from keeping the house and furnishings considerably cleaner and sweeter-smelling.

Two new warm-air systems, offering conditions close to full air-conditioning, have appeared on the market recently. The first, from Lennox Industries, can be either gas- or oil-fired and starts with a basic warm-air central heating system to which can be added four 'comfort conditioning' units. These can be installed at the outset or added later. The basic warm-air system brings the temperature up to the right level while the air circulation through the ducts creates a sufficient, though barely perceptible, air change which prevents stuffiness. You can then add a unit to de-humidify and cool the air in summer and a humidifier to moisturize the atmosphere in very dry weather. Aircraft and traffic noise can then be shut out by double-glazing the windows and keeping them closed. In this case a regulated supply of filtered, fresh air can be introduced into each room through the heating grilles to provide better ventilation. Keeping the windows closed will of course, keep out a lot of dust and dirt, but an electrostatic air filter can be added to remove virtually all dust, dirt and pollen – even cigarette smoke – from the air.

The simpler Elvaco electric system comes from Sweden, and again, is most appropriate for a house where all windows are sealed and double-glazed. It provides both heating and ventilation in winter, and in the summer the combination of good thermal insulation and ventilation provides a pleasant cool atmosphere. The ventilation part of the system consists of a fan unit inserted through an outside wall of the building. This draws in outside air, cleans it through a filter which then distributes this fresh air to room outlets through ducts made from $1\frac{1}{2}$-inch diameter rigid polythene tube. This ducting can be accommodated in the concrete of a new floor slab or in the joists of suspended floors. Each fan unit is capable of supplying 12 ducts and each duct terminates in an outlet which has a low temperature-diffuser unit mounted over it which looks like a simple wall-hung convector. A thermostat in each room keeps the temperature at whatever level is required.

The Elvaco system provides a constant supply of clean, fresh air in the house, which causes a slight over-pressure to build up within heated rooms. In turn, this induces the heated air to move towards lower-pressure areas, such as bathrooms and kitchens, to eliminate steam and cooking odours at the source; this considerably reduces condensation problems. The Elvaco system uses day-time electricity but, because of its particular efficiency, running-costs compare favourably with other systems using a cheaper fuel.

Keeping your heating under control

Human bodies do not work at their most efficient when sensing changes of temperature. Most people feel comfortable within a range of some 3°F above and 3°F below a mean temperature (about 68°–70°F in Britain at present) and will put up with temperatures a further 2°F on either side of this, before bothering to adjust the heat setting. This gives a tolerance range overall of about 10°F, whereas a sensitive thermostat can maintain the temperature output of a well-designed heating system within 2°F.

Such consistency of temperature not only adds to the comfort gained from your heating but dramatically reduces fuel costs. Running heating only 1 per cent above the temperature needed can increase fuel consumption over the year by as much as 5 per cent, so you can see how much fuel, and therefore money, can be wasted with an uncontrolled system. Good controls can reduce your heating bills by as much as 30 per cent and, if you incorporate them when you install your heating system, the size, and thus the capital cost of the installation, can be reduced as well.

Heating can be controlled both by time switches, which simply turn the output on or off, and by thermostats which control the temperature of the heat output. Time switches ensure that heating is only on when it is needed; thermostats ensure that, when the heating is on, it is at the right temperature. The most complex control systems incorporate both time switches and thermostats.

The simplest time switches can be set to turn equipment on and off for two separate periods each day, the more complicated ones will provide up to twelve separate operating periods. You can also obtain a time switch which will switch off completely for up to six days and then switch itself back on to its normal time cycle, which makes it a particularly useful device if you are often away for short periods.

Simple time controls can be extremely useful for controlling porch and drive lighting, or electric blankets, which can be switched on shortly before bedtime and turned off automatically after a pre-set interval. Similar devices can turn on a bedside lamp or a radio to wake you in the morning, or can be pre-set to turn lights off and on to fool burglars when you are away.

Time switches can control the output of water-filled radiator systems by turning on and off the pump which circulates the hot water. Except for most solid fuel boilers and some vaporizing oil ones, which have to be kept burning continuously, time switches can be used to control the domestic hot water at the same time by turning the boiler itself off and on. The heating units of warm air systems can be controlled directly in the same way.

Programmers are the most complex form of time switch for central heating and hot water. In particular they give much more control over switching on and off domestic hot water, and you should tell your heating engineer clearly the pattern of your family life so that he can select the one that will suit your requirements best.

All central heating boilers contain a thermostat, called a 'boilerstat', which controls the temperature of the water flowing through the boiler. Adjusting this manually provides the simplest means of controlling the temperature output of a hot water radiator system. However, in Britain temperature changes of as much as 20°F can easily occur in the space of a few hours. Quite apart from the difficulty of forecasting such changes, this method of control does demand a lot of attention and is, at best, a rough and ready one.

A completely automatic control which needs no knob twiddling, and is altogether far more reliable, is the 'roomstat'. A roomstat is designed to respond to the air temperature of the room it is in. When the temperature drops, it switches on the pump that circulates the hot water in a radiator system or the fan which circulates the hot air in a hot air system. When the air temperature rises to the one required in the room, the roomstat automatically switches the pump or the fan off.

Clearly, it is important to site a roomstat where it won't be affected by temperature changes peculiar to that room. A living-room with wide south-facing windows, for example, may get hot through sun penetration so that the roomstat switches off, causing the rooms in the rest of the house to become cold. Lighting a fire in such a room, or entertaining a large number of people, could have the same effect. Equally, with a roomstat in the hall, the constant opening of the front door could cause the temperature to drop there, resulting in more heat than required in the other rooms of the house.

In a flat, a single roomstat would be sufficient to give adequate temperature control throughout. But in a house, it is well worth controlling the upper and lower floors independently so that the temperatures of the bedrooms remain constant and independent of those on the floor below. The larger the house, the more zones it is worth breaking it up into; by zoning the heating, rooms can be completely switched out of the system or kept at far lower temperatures while unoccupied.

The Gas Board use roomstats in conjunction with other Honeywell controls in their Guaranteed Warmth Scheme and have demonstrated, through the remarkably low installation and running costs they have achieved, how much can be saved when a really effective system of controls is incorporated into a heating system.

Perhaps the most certain means of keeping the whole house fixed constantly at a temperature you want it is to use an outside thermostat. This is fixed in a sunless position, on a north wall of the building, and by registering outside temperature changes, it can alert the heating system so that it is prepared in advance to meet the subsequent temperature changes which will occur inside the house. Since such a system does not rely on an individual room loosing heat to set it going again, it can produce a less fluctuating level of comfort than a roomstat.

Although external sensors are probably most appropriate for larger houses in constant use, they are extremely effective employed in conjunction with electric night storage heating systems. Simple storage radiators do have manual controls but you have to guess ahead how cold or hot the coming night will be in order to adjust them, whereas an external sensor will automatically control the charging of all the storage heaters in the house, so that they will have enough heat to maintain the required room temperature throughout the following day.

If a more precise control of the radiators in individual rooms is wanted – where, for instance, one member of the family or a guest may like a very cool room at night, or when you want to keep a room aired for a period, but not to turn the heating off completely – you can use thermostatic radiator valves. These simply take the place of the standard radiator on/off knob and cost only a few pounds more each.

Where radiator heating systems are switched off regularly at night, there is always a danger of freezing and burst pipes. To prevent this there are controls, called 'frost-stats', which can either over-ride the time clock and switch on the boiler to raise the temperature of the water in the pipes, or switch on the circulating pump to keep it moving. Frost-stats are unnecessary, however, if you run your heating system continuously setting it back some 10°F lower at night than running it only during the day. Heating engineers tend to

prefer this as they feel it is better for boilers to be run at a steadier output than to be turned off completely and then run full pelt. There is virtually no difference in running costs, so it makes sense to use the system that gives the most comfort.

Many people dislike central heating simply because the air gets too dry. The warmer the air becomes, the more moisture it can carry, so that when cold frosty air is drawn into the house and heated, it tends to absorb moisture from your eyes, hair and skin, as well as from woodwork and furniture. As a result, eyes become irritated, skin gets dry, the woodwork cracks, and the piano gets out of tune in no time at all. With most warm air systems, it is possible to incorporate a humidifier the action of which is controlled by a hygrometer, so that moisture is fed into the system to give the most comfortable conditions. With radiator systems, individually-controlled room humidifiers are necessary.

More and more people are fitting double glazing in their homes, not only to prevent heat loss but to keep out the noise of traffic and aircraft. Efficiently sealing up the house in this way demands controlled ventilation, and in towns and cities this means controlling the intake of dirt as well. Filtering the grime from the atmosphere not only keeps furnishing and finishes much cleaner but can give considerable relief to people who suffer from bronchitis and asthma. There are two or three systems now on the market, one of which is able to remove up to 95 per cent of the dust and 99 per cent of the pollen.

Insulating the structure

To insulate a house efficiently is to do your modest bit for conservation, as by saving heat you reduce the rate at which the world's fuel resources are being used up, and you slow down the growing contamination of the atmosphere. But, in any case, out of sheer self-interest, there is every argument for insulation – and as much of it as possible. Don't be put off by the builder or heating contractor (who should know better) who says that an inch of quilt will be sufficient here or 2 inches of loose fill enough there. While you are at it, make a thorough and permanent job of insulating you house. It is a certain way of saving money in these inflationary times. A very small investment can bring remarkable returns, cutting the cost of a new heating installation by as much as 25 per cent and running costs up to as much as 45 per cent.

Insulation does more than prevent heat loss and save costs. It can provide positive comfort. When physical bodies are at different temperatures – and that means yourself as much as a heating unit such as a radiator – the warmer loses heat to the cooler until both reach the same temperature. If the fabric of the house is badly insulated, radiant heat will be absorbed from your body by the cold walls, floor and ceilings, so that even with an air temperature of some 70°F you will still not feel comfortable.

There are two parallel lines of action to take. The first is to prevent radiant heat being lost through the fabric of the

house. The second is to prevent warm air escaping through the cracks around badly-fitting doors and windows and up unused or overwide chimneys. In converting or modernizing a house, you have an ideal opportunity to improve its insulation, so long as you take this into consideration when you are planning structural changes as well as finishes. Structural insulation does for a house what fur-lined boots, thick coats and a warm scarf do for a person. It prevents radiant heat from escaping from the fabric of the house – the roof, the walls, the floors, the window panes.

Because most town houses and buildings in cities are built in terraces, in pairs or at least closed up against neighbours, these adjoining buildings help to insulate their side walls. There should be virtually no heat loss if your neighbouring buildings are themselves heated, but even if the building is unwarmed it will keep the house a lot warmer than if it were totally exposed.

In terraced houses, whatever their size, it is only the front and back walls – except for end houses – which are exposed to the elements. Quite often, particularly on the upper floors, the front and back walls of terraced houses are built of brickwork only 9 inches thick. You can easily measure this by opening the window and putting a tape across. Where this is the case, particularly with a room running across the front of the house, line the walls with a flexible polystyrene lining, such as Kotina, before re-papering. Or choose a finish that is both insulating and decorative in itself, such as cork or timber panelling of some kind. If the plaster is in such bad repair that it needs to be redone, you could line the outer walls with vertical tongued-and-grooved boarding. This gives not only splendid insulation but a durable and attractive permanent finish.

If you find the plaster on any outside walls in such poor condition that it has to be hacked off completely and you want a plastered surface again, you can build in valuable insulation by lining first with Fibreglass D.P. Dry Lining which only needs a skimming top coat. If the wallpaper is in good enough condition to form a base for painting or papering over, so that you don't want to disturb it, floor-to-ceiling, wall-to-wall lined curtains will do a good insulation job.

You will probably find that the walls of any extension you have are also only 9 inches thick. If this extension is going to be used for kitchens and bathrooms, it is a good argument for lining the walls with a finish which is in itself insulating and will both offset condensation and keep down heat loss. Tongued-and-grooved boarding could again be used, although sealed cork, or plain or patterned vinyl flooring either in sheet or tile form would all be suitable.

If you have a flat roof to the extension, this is unlikely to be insulated unless it was built very recently; in which case, it is worth lining the underside of the ceiling below with tongue-and-groove boarding, or ½-inch cork as a decorative finish, or with polystyrene panels before re-papering.

Town houses, particularly terraced ones, tend to be tall and narrow and this very shape provides a chimney up which warm air will rise. This makes it important that the main roof is generously insulated to prevent this warmth escaping through it and out of the house altogether. It is always a good idea to pack as much insulation into the roof as possible, to fill right up to the top of the joists with some sort of loose fill or quilt, and to stop up any gaps and cracks in the roof itself. Where you can't get into the roof space, line the ceiling below it and don't forget the one over the staircase, as this is where the heat funnels up. (See Attics.)

Banks of storage make useful insulation so if shelving, storage cupboards, etc, are set against outside walls they can help prevent heat loss. If you are fitting a pin-up board for yourself or a chalk-board for your children, make it a floor-to-ceiling panel and set this on an outside wall. Large mirrors, anything in fact that provides another layer of lining, are useful. Although the houses on either side will act as insulation there will be some heat loss to them, if your neighbours do not keep their houses as warm as you do, so party walls should also have cupboards fitted against them, providing sound as well as heat insulation.

A lot of heat can be lost through cold damp floors. I have described what can be done about them, whether they are found in the basement or ground floor, in the section on Basements.

Draught-proofing and double-glazing

Cold penetrates houses and warmth escapes from them in a great number of ways which are often forgotten. So, before tackling the important double glazing, it is worth checking through the whole house to find out which are the vulnerable points, and then to deal with them straight away.

Small gaps around doors and windows are easily dealt with on a do-it-yourself basis. Foam draught stripping, with adhesive backing, is the cheapest and easiest to apply, but not very durable, although it is useful for metal framed windows. The metal spring type of draught stripping is difficult for the layman to fix to metal windows, but easy enough with wood frames if your windows and doors fit reasonably well. However, if your windows are badly out of shape, firms such as Hermeseal and Chamberlain Weather Strips, will do a professional job for you on any kind of window – wood, metal, even aged lattice frames – which they will guarantee and should virtually last a lifetime. Ideally, draught-stripping should be carried out after all painting has been finished, the house has experienced a winter of heating, and some shrinkage has taken place.

Threshold strips under outside doors keep out rain and snow as well as cold draughts. These are made of metal, with a springy plastic central section, which is depressed by the door on shutting to form a tight seal. Sealmaster and Duraflex are the best-known of these. They are easily cut to fit the width of the door and are simply screwed into position.

Where external doors are exposed to prevailing winds, porches and greenhouses can provide useful draught-breakers. Sometimes space can be gained from an over-large or a long, narrow hall to make a draught lobby; glass doors and panels will avoid loss of light and prevent any boxy feeling. If this is not possible, an architect should be able to design a closed porch appropriate to the character and period of the house. Greenhouses and conservatories will do the same useful job, where french, garden or back doors open into them. Roofing over and fitting doors at each end of the space between a side door and an adjacent garage is another simple way of providing such a wind-break.

If you have decided to keep an open fire in the sitting-room, you should check its flue. Over-wide flues are often culprits so far as heat-loss is concerned, and throat restricters, obtainable from builders' merchants, will considerably reduce the flow of warm air from the room. Some form of under-floor draught is equally successful, as this supports combustion at the hearth and so prevents warm air from being drawn from the room itself for this purpose. Ducts for under-floor draughts are not difficult to run between the joists of suspended floors. If you decide to hang on to a handsome old fireplace, without ever using it to light a fire, and you have some other form of ventilation or air conditioning, it is worth blocking off the flue during the winter months. However, where you have draught-stripped and double-glazed windows against noise and cold it might be better to leave the fireplace open or, if you do block it, to fit a 'hit and miss' ventilator in its flue, in order to achieve some sort of ventilation or air movement.

Extractor fans in bathrooms, kitchens and utility rooms, where fumes or steam are generated, will keep the air fresh and avoid the need for open windows. An extractor fan venting to the outside is to be preferred to the ductless hoods designed to hang over cookers. They are much more effective.

Having draught-stripped the windows, well-fitting blinds and heavy floor-to-ceiling curtains can do a lot to prevent heat loss during all but the short daylight hours in winter. Wooden shutters are even better and are well worth putting into order if your house is lucky enough to have them, so be sure you haven't one tucked in the panel below sash windows. However, double glazing can provide a higher level of heat insulation, freedom from condensation and protection from outside noise.

Preventing condensation on window panes does stop the deterioration of the paint work on the frames and the steaming up of the glass itself, so that pools of water on the window-sill become a thing of the past. At the same time, you should try to tackle the problem at source by providing adequate ventilation and sufficient background heat to prevent the air dropping its moisture content on any cold surface.

Protection from outside noise is particularly valuable for people living in towns and cities. Even the small space between the two sheets of glass in a double glazing panel will do something to flatten off the high notes, although to be really effective the minimum air space needs to be about 4 inches, and the optimum about 12 inches. It is essential that the window frames are sealed tightly so that no sound can penetrate through air gaps. In some cases it is an advantage to line the reveals between the window frame and the double glazing frame with a sound-absorbent material. but if soundproofing is a particular problem in your house, it is important to go to a firm who specializes in this particular application of double glazing.

A further advantage of double glazing or any other kind of adequate window insulation is the opportunity to use the entire room. The areas next to large windows are no longer chillier than the rest of the room, and there is no need to huddle around the fire or the largest radiator. A reliable figure on the amount of heat double glazing can save is given by the Insulating Glazing Association – the trade organization concerned with maintaining and improving standards of double glazing. As a result of a nation-wide survey they found that an average saving of $22\frac{1}{2}$ per cent on fuel bills can be achieved.

Factory-sealed units come in two versions, both looking like a single sheet of glass with only two faces to clean. Both are hermetically-sealed to avoid any misting up between the panes. The units start from $\frac{5}{8}$-inch thick, although wider units are available, and even multiple ones incorporating triple glazing, such as those used in an office block about 300 yards from a runway at Manchester Airport. With both kinds of units, draught stripping of the window frame is essential. In one version, the two sheets of glass are held together with a sealed metal, alloy or plastic edge and separated by a spacer. Units of this type are usually purpose-made and require a deeper rebate than the other type which is all glass. These units are made by moulding and fusing the edges of two sheets of glass, withdrawing the moist air between the inner surfaces and then sealing it off. They are available in standard sizes to match many ranges of standard windows.

Double-glazing panels are worth considering if you are having to fit new windows anyway, as this will avoid fitting a second frame for the double glazing. However, the heat loss is rather higher and noise prevention rather lower than with the following types, unless you install a unit incorporating three sheets of glass – triple glazing. Most window ranges are now made with a deep enough rebate to take double glazing panels – but this should be checked.

Coupled sashes are generally made in timber and are very popular with the Scandinavians. There are several makes available in this country, but this is essentially an application where new windows are being made or old ones replaced. It consists of one single glazed window with second sash coupled to the main sash allowing both sashes to move together. The second sash is fitted with hinges and fasteners so that the two glass faces can be separated for cleaning purposes. The air space between the panes in this system is usually enough to give useful sound insulation. Blinds can be fitted between the frames if required, and again draught stripping of the main frame is essential. However, this is usually built in by the manufacturers.

The term 'secondary' windows covers a wide range of systems, in which a second frame is attached to the existing window frame or is separate from it but within the same window opening. The greater the distance between the frames, the better the sound insulation, and usually these are the most effective systems where sound insulation is the priority. Some are made completely in lightweight aluminium; others are in aluminium framed in hardwood to ensure rigidity and a perfect fit. There are also rigid plastic versions made to measure, or systems consisting of plastic extrusions, which can be easily cut to length and incorporate corner fittings to hold the panes together. They are available in several variations – fixed, sliding or hinged to allow for ventilation. The glazed secondary frame is usually removable for cleaning. Some manufacturers provide an installation service, but those who do not usually supply comprehensive fixing instructions.

Do-it-yourself kits come in the secondary window category and are even simpler and cheaper for the do-it-yourself enthusiast, as they use flexible plastic channels to hold the second pane of glass. The glass itself can be obtained, cut to size, from your local builders' merchants. Special clips and screws are provided and, after the glass has been fixed inside the panel, it is a simple matter to fix the secondary window to the main window frame. Most manufacturers provide assembly and fixing instructions.

In deciding which windows to double glaze, those facing north and east should take priority – clearly the larger the window, the greater the benefit. You may find that there are some windows you never open from one year's end to the next, or at least never in the winter, in which case a simple do-it-yourself kit which blocks off the entire window would be adequate. Where you need moving sashes, make it clear to the firm you employ that the frames of the double glazing sashes must coincide exactly with those of the existing windows.

Roof lights are often a great source of heat loss and are always worth double glazing. Where they don't have to be opened during the winter months, a simple do-it-yourself system could seal them off, but if you need to fit a new one, the type made by Velux is well worth considering. It com-

prises two linked sashes, between which blinds can be fitted, and gives good insulation against both heat and noise. It has its own prefabricated flashing and, as far as I know, never leaks.

If you do consider double glazing, avoid the cut-price firms who come knocking at doors. The Insulation Glazing Association will send you a list of manufacturers and installers of every kind, as well as prices for each system. From these firms, you will receive a guarantee of workmanship and reliable opportunity for redress should anything go wrong.

Although Rentokil are not members of the IGA, they provide a really professional whole-house insulation service, with a long-term guarantee. They not only make double glazing units, but will install sliding secondary sashes, draught stripping, cavity filling, roof insulation, etc, and can advise what is most appropriate to your particular house and pocket.

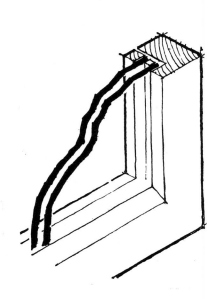

Factory-sealed double-glazing units are almost like a single pane of glass. Here, the two panes are held together by metal or plastic and are hermetically sealed

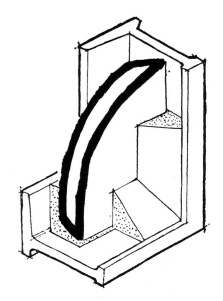

Another type of factory-sealed unit, made from all glass. Two pieces of glass are moulded together and the air between removed

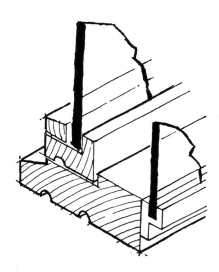

Double-glazing for coupled sashes: this allows for an auxiliary window to be coupled to the existing one, the two moving together

INDEX

207

USEFUL ADDRESSES

British Carpet Centre, Dorland House, 14 Lower Regent Street, London SW1

British Ceramic Tile Council, Federation House, Stoke-on-Trent, ST4 2RU

British Standards Institution, 2 Park Street, London W1

Building Centre, 26 Store Street, Tottenham Court Road, London WC1

Bristol Building Centre Limited, Stonebridge House, Colston Avenue, Bristol 1

Building Information Centre, 16 Trumpington Street, Cambridge

Engineering and Building Centre, Broad Street, Birmingham 1

Manchester Building Centre, 113 Portland Street, Manchester 1

Midland Design and Building Centre, Mansfield Road, Nottingham

Scottish Building Centre, 425 Sauchiehall Street, Glasgow C2

Calor Gas Sales and Service, 21A Avenue Road, London N14

Cement and Concrete Association, 52 Grosvenor Gardens, London SW1

Chartered Auctioneers' and Estate Agents' Institute, 29 Lincoln's Inn Fields, London WC2

Chartered Land Agents' Society, 21 Lincoln's Inn Fields, London WC2

Church Commissioners for England, 1 Millbank, London SW1

Coal Utilization Council, 19 Rochester Row, London SW1

Consumers' Association, 14 Buckingham Street, London WC2

Crown Commissioners, Crown Commissioners' Estate Office, Whitehall, London SW1

Design Council, 28 Haymarket, London W1

Scottish Design Council, 72 St Vincent Street, Glasgow C2

Electrical Contractors' Association, 55 Catherine Place, London SW1

Electricity Council, 30 Millbank, London SW1

Electricity Council Marketing, Trafalgar Buildings, 1 Charing Cross Road, London SW1

Gas Council, 59 Bryanston Street, London W1

Georgian Group, 2 Chester Street, London SW1

Heating and Ventilating Contractors Association, Coastal Chambers, Buckingham Palace Road, London SW1

Historical Buildings Bureau, Ministry of Housing, Queen Anne's Mansions, Queen Anne's Gate, London SW1

Incorporated Society of Valuers and Auctioneers, 3 Cadogan Gate, London SW1

Institute of Landscape Architects, 38 Russell Square, London WC1

Institution of Heating and Ventilating Engineers, 49 Cadogan Square, London SW1

Insulation and Glazing Association, 6 Mount Row, London W1

Land Registry, HM, Lincoln's Inn Fields, London WC1

Master Builders' Federation, 33 John Street, London WC1

National Heating Centre, 34 Mortimer Street, London W1

National House-Builders' Registration Council, 58 Portland Place, London W1

Royal Institute of British Architects, 66 Portland Place, London W1

Royal Institute of Chartered Surveyors, 12 Great George Street, London SW1

Society for the Protection of Ancient Buildings, 55 Great Ormond Street, London WC1

Timber Research and Development Association Limited, 26 Store Street, London WC1

'WHICH' Advice Centre, 242 Kentish Town Road, London NW5